WHAT'S IN YOUR BASKET?

THE CHOPPED
COOKBOOK

THE CHOPPED COOKBOOK

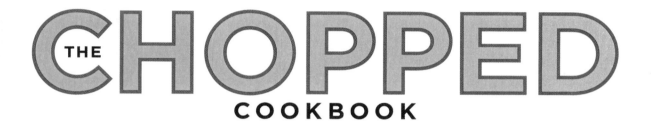

USE WHAT YOU'VE GOT TO COOK SOMETHING GREAT

CLARKSON POTTER/PUBLISHERS
NEW YORK

Published in the United States by Clarkson Potter/Publishers,
an imprint of the Crown Publishing Group, a division of Random House LLC, a Penguin Random House Company, New York.
www.crownpublishing.com
www.clarksonpotter.com

Library of Congress Cataloging-in-Publication Data

The chopped cookbook / Food Network Kitchen. — First edition.
pages cm
Includes index.
(hardback) 1. Cooking. I. Food Network (Firm)
TX714.C494 2014
641.5—dc23 2013037025

ISBN 978-0-7704-3500-4
eBook ISBN 978-0-7704-3501-1

Printed in the United States of America

Book design by Jennifer K. Beal Davis for Ballast Design
Jacket design by Marysarah Quinn
Photography by Armando Rafael Moutela

10 9 8 7 6 5 4 3 2 1

First Edition

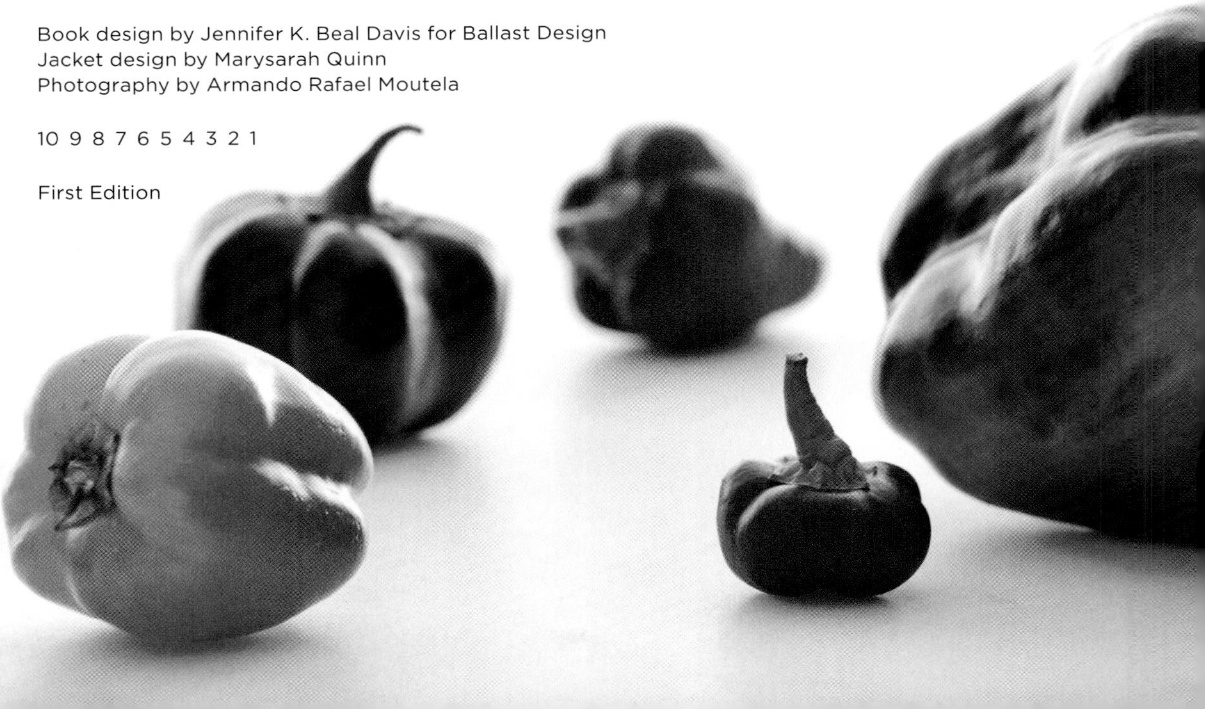

TO ALL THE CHEFS WHO HAVE PASSED THROUGH OUR KITCHEN THROUGHOUT THE MANY YEARS OF *CHOPPED*: THANK YOU FOR YOUR CREATIVITY AND FEARLESSNESS. YOU INSPIRE OUR COOKING DAILY.

CONTENTS

INTRODUCTION 8

THE CHOPPED PANTRY 12

PASTA NIGHT 17

CHICKENS GONE WILD 39

EGGS AFTER BREAKFAST 63

FLASH IN THE PAN 83

COMPLETELY FUN WAYS TO COOK VEGETABLES 111

ALL THINGS GROUND: BEYOND BEEF 139

BIG SALADS: HEARTY AND FRESH 159

FISHING FOR COMPLIMENTS 177

GREAT GRAINS 197

SHORT AND SWEET: EASY DESSERTS 219

ACKNOWLEDGMENTS 234

INDEX 235

INTRO-
DUCTION

A *CHOPPED* COOKBOOK? Like the Food Network show where chefs make three dishes in almost no time with crazy ingredients? Well, sort of. We've all been there—you open your fridge on a Tuesday night to be faced with ground turkey, a pineapple, and seafood seasoning, along with thirty minutes or so before dinner needs to be on the table. (For that particular combo, turn to page 155 to find the recipe for Thai Turkey Lettuce Wraps.)

But this book does away with the fish heads and gummy worms and, instead, focuses on ingredients most Americans tend to buy every week at the supermarket. It boldly aims to solve the nightly "what's for dinner?" conundrum and help you get excited about boneless chicken breasts again.

That's what we're here for. Our Food Network Kitchen is made up of chefs, stylists, recipe developers, researchers, and all-around food nerds—we're the culinary engine behind your favorite Food Network shows and websites, plus the magazine, wines, restaurants, cooking tools, and more. We're the ones who select the baskets of ingredients for the hit show *Chopped*, and we make sure that each basket, no matter how wacky, has many delicious potential outcomes.

The thrill of peering into the refrigerator to see what you've got for dinner was the original inspiration for *Chopped*. Twenty-one seasons later, we've seen some amazing cooking and enormous ingenuity under pressure. This book is our way of bringing all of that back home, only with ingredients most of us usually have on hand. The joy of *Chopped* comes from watching talented chefs be inspired by the food in front of them. We're hoping that this book gets you inspired as well.

In these pages, you'll find new and tasty ways of looking at your groceries, with challenges sprinkled throughout, plus a ton of things to do with that one vegetable left in your crisper at the end of the week and behind-the-scenes insight from your favorite *Chopped* judges. We held grueling twice-a-day tastings (yeah, it's a tough job) and battled it out until we agreed on the best, most doable, and delicious recipes. Tucked into each chapter is a bonus section: a few ways to spin an old favorite, a chart of mix-and-match sauces or dressings, or a market basket challenge, where we gave teams a four-item basket and then devoured the different results.

So use this book to help you look at familiar ingredients in new ways—and, most important, to have fun while getting a delicious dinner on the table.

CHEFS, OPEN YOUR BASKETS!

PHILLY-STYLE GARLICKY GREENS AND EGG SANDWICH, PAGE 74

THE CHOPPED PANTRY

The *Chopped* show pantry is vast and deep; it includes seven vinegars, three different kinds of gelatin, and five kinds of salt. You don't need all that. What you do need (and what we're here to help with) is a sense of how foods work, and how one ingredient can be substituted for another, so you can use what you have on hand to cook what you want to make.

We want you to feel comfortable improvising. To that end, we've organized our pantry a bit differently. So while our "Basics" category is straightforward, the majority of these groupings (like "Richness" and "Crunch") function more as a guide to an ingredient's role in a dish. If something calls for almonds, but you're out of them, you can swap in peanuts or pumpkin seeds for crunch instead. If there's a salmon steak recipe you want to try but the market is all out of salmon, try it with a different fish. If you love sour cream but don't love Greek yogurt, by all means use sour cream! And if a recipe calls for lemon juice and you feel like mixing it up, try cider vinegar or even pickle juice. If you think, "Hmm, this could be a little brighter," then you know anything under "Acidity" will work to bring that to the table. Consider this permission to play with your food; you just might invent your next family classic with a secret ingredient.

Finally, just to reiterate: You definitely don't need every single thing on this list.

WHAT MAKES A WINNING DISH?

When we judge a recipe in the kitchen it's not just about taste. It's about the ingredients themselves and how they play off each other. It's a question of texture, balance, color, chemistry, and surprise. For example: **Creamy + a touch of acidity = balanced richness** (like cream sauce with a squeeze of lemon on pasta). **Tart + fruit or herbal = bright** (like lemon juice and oil on salad greens). **Vegetables with a swirl of lushness = smooth and rounded** (like mashed potatoes with melted butter). **Crunchy + juicy = comforting** (like battered onion rings).

BASICS

- **Eggs**, large
- **Milk**, whole or 2%
- **Unsalted butter** (we'd rather add the salt ourselves)
- **Oil**, including extra-virgin olive oil (for dressing) and vegetable oil (for cooking)
- **Vinegar** (see Acidity for options)
- **Salt**, both fine (for baking) and kosher (for everything else)
- **Black peppercorns** (buy whole ones and grind as you go)
- **Flour** (see Baking Basics)
- **Sugar** (see Sweetness for options)
- **Potatoes**, red or russet
- **Garlic**
- **Ginger**
- **Bell peppers**
- **Carrots**
- **Celery**
- **Onions** or **scallions**
- **Romaine hearts**
- **Tomatoes**
- Fresh **flat-leaf parsley**
- Fresh **cilantro**
- Fresh **thyme**

RICHNESS

- **Cheese**, such as Parmesan, Cheddar, or shredded mozzarella
- **Greek yogurt** or **sour cream**
- **Mayonnaise**
- **Nut butter**
- **Toasted sesame oil** (for seasoning; this is one of our secret ingredients, transforming whatever it touches into more than the sum of its parts)

SWEETNESS

- **Dried fruit**
- **Honey**
- **Jelly**, **jam**, or **preserves**
- **Maple syrup**
- **Sugar**, brown, confectioners', and granulated

CRUNCH

- **Nuts**, such as almonds, walnuts, pecans, or peanuts
- **Breading**, including panko or plain dry bread crumbs, cornmeal, rice cereal, and crackers
- **Seeds**, sunflower or pumpkin

ACIDITY

- **Balsamic vinegar** (has a touch of sweetness)
- **Cider vinegar** (tart)
- **Red wine vinegar** (a good all-around choice)
- **Rice vinegar** (mild)
- **Lemons** or **limes** (fresh and powerful)

SALTINESS AND SAVORINESS

(these add big flavor and depth):

- **Anchovy fillets**
- **Asian fish sauce**
- **Bacon** or **salami** or other cured meat
- **Olives** or **capers**
- **Soy sauce** or **tamari** (tamari is more flavorful and wheat free)
- **Tomato paste**
- **Worcestershire sauce**

TANGINESS

- **Barbecue sauce**
- **Ketchup**
- **Mustard**, both Dijon and whole grain
- **Pickles**, sweet or dill

SPICE/HEAT

- **Chiles**, such as chipotles in adobo or pickled jalapeños
- **Hot sauce**, such as Tabasco, Sriracha, and sambal (we love garlicky, tart Asian-style sauces)
- **Salsa**

BROTHINESS

- **Chicken broth**
- **Coconut milk**
- **Tomatoes**, fresh or canned: whole, crushed, or diced

BAKING BASICS

- **Flour** (all-purpose and whole wheat)
- **Baking powder**
- **Baking soda**
- **Cookies**, such as chocolate wafers and shortbread
- **Cornstarch** (to thicken sauces or dry things out before frying)
- **Instant coffee**
- **Refrigerated pie dough**
- **Rolled oats**
- **Vanilla extract**
- **Unsweetened cocoa powder** (also great in savory foods to add richness and sweetness)

FROZEN BASICS

- **Dough**, both puff pastry and pizza (for last-minute appetizers, and to give leftovers a new life)
- **Fruit**, such as berries, peaches, and mangoes
- **Vanilla ice cream**
- **Vegetables**, including peas, corn, spinach, and kale

STARCHES

- **Bread**
- **Canned beans**, such as chickpeas, cannellini, black, or pinto
- **Couscous**
- **Pasta and noodles**, with different shapes of wheat, rice, and egg types
- **Quinoa**
- **Rice**, medium- or long-grain
- **Tortillas**, corn or flour

SINGLE SPICES

- **Bay leaves**
- **Cayenne pepper**
- **Chile powder** (made from one kind of pepper, such as ancho, or a blend; see Spice Blends)
- **Cinnamon**, ground
- **Coriander**, ground
- **Cumin**, ground
- **Dill seed**
- **Fennel seed**
- **Nutmeg**, whole (grate it as you need it)
- **Oregano**, dried
- **Paprika**, sweet and smoked
- **Red pepper** flakes, crushed

SPICE BLENDS

- **Cajun seasoning**
- **Chile powder** (a blend and individual chile powders, as you see fit)
- **Chinese five-spice powder** (a workhorse with a bit of mystery)
- **Jerk seasoning**
- **Madras curry powder**
- **Seafood seasoning**, like Old Bay

SAY UMAMI

You know how Worcestershire sauce adds punch to a Bloody Mary? That's umami. As we cook, we often find ourselves turning to Asian fish sauce and anchovies to amp things up. We use them for a big flavor boost stirred into a tomato sauce, a stew, a stir-fry, or a dressing, bringing not-necessarily-fishy intensity to the foods around them. If your first reaction is "ew," make yourself try them in the recipe anyway. You won't taste fish; you'll just taste all of the other flavors so much more. Look for lighter-colored fish sauce (lightness is a sign of freshness and higher quality) in the Asian section of your grocery store.

PASTA
NIGHT

A box of pasta in your pantry means you're already halfway to dinner. Whether you have two other ingredients or ten, here's how to turn them into quick comfort.

SPAGHETTI WITH TOMATO CARBONARA

ORECCHIETTE WITH GARLIC,
CAPERS, AND BREAD CRUMBS

SPINACH AND ARTICHOKE DIP
MAC AND CHEESE

MEXICAN SPAGHETTI AND MEATBALLS

PENNE ALLA MARY

PLAY WITH YOUR PASTA

TORTELLINI WITH CREAM CHEESE
ALFREDO AND PEAS

RIGATONI WITH SPICY SAUSAGE
AND CRISPY MUSHROOMS

CHILLED PEANUT CHICKEN
NOODLE SALAD

LINGUINE WITH BELL PEPPER MARINARA

FARFALLE WITH EGGPLANT
YOGURT SAUCE

SPAGHETTI WITH TOMATO CARBONARA

Carbonara might be meant for pasta, but *Chopped* chefs have used it well for both smoked fish and fiddlehead ferns. The lesson here? Bacon + eggs + cheese = delicious, no matter what you add them to. In this take, tomato paste adds warmth and depth without adding liquid.

Kosher salt

5 slices **bacon**, chopped

1 small **onion**, chopped (about ¼ cup)

2 tablespoons **tomato paste**

1 pound **spaghetti**

3 large **eggs**

¾ cup grated **Parmesan**, plus more for serving

3 tablespoons chopped fresh **flat-leaf parsley leaves**

Freshly ground **black pepper**

START THE WATER: Bring a large pot of salted water to a boil.

PREP THE SAUCE: Put the bacon in a cold large skillet and cook over medium heat, stirring occasionally, until crisp, about 10 minutes. Transfer to a bowl using a slotted spoon. Add the onion to the bacon fat and cook until soft, about 5 minutes. Add the tomato paste and cook, stirring, until a shade darker, about 1 minute. Remove the skillet from the heat and reserve.

COOK THE PASTA: Add the pasta to the boiling water and cook according to package directions. Reserve 1 cup of the cooking water, then drain the pasta.

TOSS AND SERVE: Return the skillet to low heat. Whisk the eggs and Parmesan in a medium bowl. Add the beaten eggs, pasta, and half of the reserved cooking water to the skillet. Cook, stirring continuously, until the eggs are thickened and cooked but not curdled, about 2 minutes. Add the bacon, parsley, and more reserved pasta water until the pasta is creamy and the sauce coats the pasta. Season with salt and pepper and serve with additional cheese.

To quickly peel a whole head of **GARLIC**, smash it firmly with your hand to separate the cloves, then place into a large pot with a lid and shake vigorously for 15 seconds. The cloves can then be picked from the skins.

ORECCHIETTE with GARLIC, CAPERS, and BREAD CRUMBS

Slowly cooking garlic in olive oil lends a mellow, almost-sweet flavor to this sauce, while homemade coarse bread crumbs bring crunch to every bite.

1 head **garlic**, separated into cloves and peeled
½ cup **extra-virgin olive oil**
Kosher salt
1 cup cubed crusty **Italian bread**
1 **anchovy fillet**, chopped
¼ cup drained and chopped brined **capers**
½ teaspoon crushed **red pepper flakes**
Freshly ground **black pepper**
1 pound **orecchiette**
½ cup grated **Parmesan**
½ cup fresh **flat-leaf parsley leaves**

COOK THE GARLIC: Combine the garlic, oil, and ¼ teaspoon salt in a medium skillet over medium-low heat and cook, stirring frequently, until the garlic is golden and tender, about 25 minutes. Transfer the garlic to a bowl using a slotted spoon and smash with a fork.

START THE WATER: Bring a large pot of salted water to a boil.

TOAST THE BREAD CRUMBS: Add the bread to the skillet and cook, stirring occasionally, until golden, about 5 minutes. Transfer to a bowl using a slotted spoon. Cool and then crush into crumbs.

START THE SAUCE: Stir the anchovy into the skillet until dissolved. Remove the skillet from the heat and stir in the capers, red pepper flakes, mashed garlic, and a couple turns of pepper.

COOK THE PASTA AND TOSS: Add the pasta to the boiling water and cook according to package directions. Reserve 1 cup of the cooking water, then drain the pasta. Add the pasta to the skillet with the cooking water and cheese. Toss to coat. Sprinkle the parsley and bread crumbs over the top and serve.

SERVES 8

ACTIVE TIME

20 minutes

TOTAL TIME

1 hour
15 minutes

SPINACH AND ARTICHOKE DIP MAC AND CHEESE

What happens when two delicious dishes meet? This. Spinach-artichoke dip, in all its bubbly, cheesy glory, meets mac and cheese in all of its, well, bubbly, cheesy glory. It's a match made in heaven.

Kosher salt
4 tablespoons (½ stick) **unsalted butter**
1 large **onion**, chopped
Finely ground **black pepper**
⅓ cup **all-purpose flour**
6 cups **milk**
1 (10-ounce) package frozen **spinach**, thawed and drained
1 (9-ounce) package frozen **artichoke hearts**, thawed and drained
1¾ cups shredded **mozzarella** (about 7 ounces)
1 pound **elbow pasta**
1 cup **panko bread crumbs**
2 tablespoons **extra-virgin olive oil**

SET UP: Preheat the oven to 400°F.

START THE WATER: Bring a large pot of salted water to a boil.

MAKE THE SAUCE: Heat the butter in a medium saucepan over medium-high heat. Stir in the onion, 2½ teaspoons salt, and a couple turns of pepper and cook, stirring occasionally, until golden, about 6 minutes. Stir in the flour until combined. Whisk in the milk and bring to a simmer. Stir in the spinach and artichoke hearts and simmer until thickened, about 10 minutes. Stir in the mozzarella and remove from the heat.

COOK THE PASTA: Add the pasta to the boiling water and cook according to package directions. Drain, then toss the pasta with the sauce. Transfer to a 3½-quart baking dish.

TOP AND BAKE: Toss the panko with the oil and sprinkle over the pasta. Bake until the filling is bubbling and the panko is golden, about 40 minutes.

SERVES 4

ACTIVE TIME

35 minutes

TOTAL TIME

45 minutes

MEXICAN SPAGHETTI
AND MEATBALLS

Spicy tomato-chile sauce takes spaghetti on a trip around the world in this hearty Tex-Mex-meets-Spain one-skillet meal. Fideos, ultra-thin Spanish noodles, are a great choice if you can find them; we opted for more common vermicelli here.

1 pound **meatloaf mix** (ground pork, veal, and beef)

½ cup plain **dry bread crumbs**

1 large **egg**

1 tablespoon **chile powder**

2 teaspoons dried **oregano**

Kosher salt and freshly ground **black pepper**

5 tablespoons **vegetable oil**

2 **garlic cloves**, minced

1 medium **onion**, sliced

8 ounces **vermicelli noodles**, broken in half

1 (14.5-ounce) can diced **tomatoes**

½ cup crumbled **queso fresco** (about 2 ounces)

½ cup loosely packed fresh **cilantro leaves**, roughly chopped

MAKE THE MEATBALLS: Gently mix the meat, bread crumbs, egg, 2 teaspoons of the chile powder, 1 teaspoon of the oregano, ½ teaspoon salt, and a couple turns of pepper. Form heaping tablespoons into about 24 meatballs.

FRY THE MEATBALLS: Heat a large nonstick skillet over medium-high heat. When hot, pour in 2 tablespoons of the oil. Add half the meatballs and cook, turning often, to brown all sides, about 5 minutes. Transfer to a paper-towel-lined plate. Add 1 more tablespoon of the oil and repeat with the rest of the meatballs.

(continued)

COOK THE NOODLES: Add the remaining 2 tablespoons oil to the skillet. Add the garlic and onion and cook until they begin to soften, about 8 minutes. Stir in the remaining 1 teaspoon each chile powder and oregano, 1 teaspoon salt, and a couple turns of pepper. Add the noodles. Cook, stirring, until the noodles begin to brown and crisp, about 3 minutes. Stir in the diced tomatoes and their juices, 2 cups water, and the meatballs. Bring to a simmer, cover, and cook until the noodles are tender, 8 to 10 minutes.

SERVE: Spoon the noodles and meatballs into shallow bowls or onto plates. Top with queso fresco and sprinkle with cilantro.

Swap out the spices, herbs, and cheese to change up this homey, satisfying pasta dish. For a **GREEK** feel, omit the chile powder, switch the vegetable oil to **olive oil,** and finish off with **feta** and **dill** in place of the queso fresco and cilantro. To make it **ASIAN,** use 2 teaspoons **five-spice powder** in place of the chile powder, switch out the oregano for finely grated **ginger,** and serve with **hoisin sauce** instead of cheese.

SERVES 4 TO 6

ACTIVE TIME

20 minutes

TOTAL TIME

40 minutes

Add **VODKA** to the pan off the heat (and never straight from the bottle), then tip the pan so the vodka catches fire if you have a gas burner. If you'd rather not ignite the vodka (or cook on electric), feel free to cook it down instead, simmering it for 2 minutes before adding the tomatoes.

PENNE ALLA MARY

How can you make penne alla vodka even more fun? Spike it with celery and horseradish to bring the classic flavors of a Bloody Mary to dinner.

Kosher salt
¼ cup **extra-virgin olive oil**
2 to 3 **celery stalks**, chopped (about 1 cup), with some leaves reserved
2 **garlic cloves**, finely chopped
1 medium **red onion**, chopped
Freshly ground **black pepper**
2 tablespoons **vodka**
6 medium **tomatoes**, diced (about 6 cups)
3 tablespoons drained brined **capers**, plus 1 tablespoon brine
2 tablespoons **prepared horseradish**, with juice
1 tablespoon **Worcestershire sauce**
1 pound **penne**
¼ cup grated **Parmesan**

START THE WATER: Bring a large pot of salted water to a boil.

SAUTÉ THE AROMATICS: Heat the oil in a large skillet over medium-high heat. Stir in the celery, garlic, onion, 1 teaspoon salt, and a couple turns of pepper and cook, stirring occasionally, until golden, about 6 minutes.

MAKE THE SAUCE: Pull the skillet off the heat, add the vodka, return to the heat, and tip the pan to ignite on a gas flame (or light with a stick lighter); let the flames cook off, about 1 minute. Stir in ½ cup water, the tomatoes, capers and brine, horseradish, and Worcestershire. Cook, covered, over medium heat, stirring once in a while, until the tomatoes soften, about 20 minutes. Remove the lid and continue cooking for an additional 2 minutes. Season with salt and pepper. Keep the sauce warm while cooking the pasta.

COOK THE PASTA AND TOSS: Add the pasta to the boiling water and cook according to package directions. Drain the pasta and toss with the sauce. Sprinkle with the Parmesan and celery leaves.

PLAY WITH YOUR
PASTA

Often, the tastiest pasta sauce is also the simplest. Start
with a pound of spaghetti, and take it in a delicious
direction with one of our favorite three-ingredient sauces
that go from zero to dinner in minutes.

1 **BRING** a large pot of salted water to a boil. Add 1 pound **spaghetti** to the boiling water and cook according to package directions. Drain, reserving some of the pasta cooking water.

2 **THEN** choose one of these combinations:

SERVES 6

ACTIVE TIME

10 minutes

TOTAL TIME

20 minutes

LEMONY RICOTTA SAUCE

In a large bowl, stir together 1 pound **ricotta,** the grated zest of 1 **lemon,** 2 tablespoons fresh lemon juice, and ½ teaspoon each **kosher salt** and freshly ground **black pepper.** Whisk in ½ cup pasta cooking water and 1½ cups baby **arugula.** Toss with the pasta.

QUICK AND EASY MARINARA

Puree one 32-ounce can **whole tomatoes** with juice in a blender with 3 **garlic cloves**, 1 teaspoon **kosher salt,** and a couple turns of freshly ground **black pepper.** Heat ¼ cup **extra-virgin olive oil** in a large heavy skillet over medium-high heat. Carefully pour the tomato puree into the hot oil and cook, stirring occasionally, until slightly thickened, about 5 minutes. Toss with the pasta. Serve with grated **Parmesan.**

CLASSIC CHEESE AND PEPPER (CACIO E PEPE)

Heat ¼ cup **extra-virgin olive oil** in a large heavy skillet over medium-high heat. Stir in 1 tablespoon crushed **black peppercorns** and cook, stirring, until fragrant, 1 to 2 minutes. Stir in the pasta and 1½ cups pasta cooking water. Slowly add 2½ cups grated **Parmesan** and stir until the pasta is coated. Season with **kosher salt.**

GRAPE TOMATO–HERB SAUCE

Stir together 4 cups (2 pints) halved **grape tomatoes** with 3 tablespoons **extra-virgin olive oil,** 1 teaspoon **kosher salt,** a couple turns of freshly ground **black pepper,** and 2 cups chopped mixed **herbs** (such as parsley, basil, dill, cilantro, chives, or scallions) in a large bowl. Stir in the pasta and ¾ cup pasta cooking water.

TUNA AND MINT PASTA

Stir together 12 ounces **tuna** packed in extra-virgin olive oil (with the oil) and 1 finely chopped **shallot.** Season with **kosher salt** and freshly ground **black pepper.** Stir in the pasta, ¾ cup pasta cooking water, and 1 cup torn fresh **mint leaves.**

3 **SEASON** with salt and pepper (or just salt, for the Cacio e Pepe).

TORTELLINI WITH CREAM CHEESE ALFREDO AND PEAS

Whisk cream cheese into milk for a creamy, cheesy Alfredo sauce that comes together in minutes. If you don't have tortellini, no worries—this works just as well over any other pasta.

Kosher salt
1½ cups **milk**
8 ounces **cream cheese**
½ cup grated **Parmesan**, plus more for serving
Coarsely ground **black pepper**
2 cups frozen **peas**, thawed
1 cup diced **ham**
18 ounces **cheese tortellini** (two 9-ounce packages)

START THE WATER: Bring a large pot of salted water to a boil.

MAKE THE SAUCE: Bring the milk, cream cheese, and Parmesan to a simmer in a large saucepan, whisking vigorously until the cream cheese is dissolved and the sauce is thickened, about 5 minutes. Season with ½ teaspoon salt and a couple turns of pepper. Stir in the peas, remove from the heat, and stir in the ham.

COOK THE PASTA AND TOSS: Add the pasta to the boiling water and cook according to package directions. Drain the pasta and toss with the sauce. Season with salt and pepper, sprinkle with additional Parmesan, and serve immediately.

RIGATONI WITH SPICY SAUSAGE AND CRISPY MUSHROOMS

Roasting mushrooms concentrates their flavor, adding deep savoriness to this dish. Starting with packaged sliced mushrooms saves you precious minutes of prep time. Get these right in the oven as soon as you walk in the door.

Kosher salt

1 pound **button mushrooms**, sliced ¼ inch thick

¼ cup **extra-virgin olive oil**

1 teaspoon chopped fresh **rosemary**, plus 1 small sprig

Freshly ground **black pepper**

12 ounces spicy or sweet **Italian sausage** (about 4 links), casings removed

2 **garlic cloves**, thinly sliced

1 (28-ounce) can crushed **tomatoes**

1 pound **rigatoni**

Grated **Gruyère**, **Parmesan**, or **pecorino**, for serving

SET UP: Preheat the oven to 375°F and bring a large pot of salted water to a boil.

ROAST THE MUSHROOMS: Toss the mushrooms with 3 tablespoons of the oil, the chopped rosemary, 1 teaspoon salt, and a couple turns of pepper. Lay on a baking sheet in one layer and roast, stirring occasionally, until mostly dry and crisp in places, 40 to 50 minutes.

SIMMER THE SAUCE: While the mushrooms get crispy, heat the remaining tablespoon oil in a medium saucepan over medium-high heat. Add the sausage and garlic and cook, breaking up the clumps with a wooden spoon, until brown, about 6 minutes. Add the crushed tomatoes with their juices, the rosemary sprig, and 1 cup water and bring to a simmer. Reduce the heat to medium and cook, stirring occasionally, until slightly thickened, about 15 minutes. Season with salt and pepper.

COOK THE PASTA AND TOSS: Add the pasta to the boiling water and cook according to package directions. Transfer the pasta to a large serving bowl and toss with the sausage sauce. Discard the rosemary. Serve topped with the mushrooms and grated cheese.

PERSIAN CUKES
have a thin skin and
a delicate flavor.
Because their skins
are so thin, you don't
have to peel them,
and they're almost
seedless, so you
don't need to seed
them either. If you
can't find them, use
a regular cucumber
instead, and peel
and seed it.

CHILLED PEANUT CHICKEN NOODLE SALAD

Poaching chicken in a peanut butter broth brings nuttiness into each bite. The flavorful poaching liquid then becomes the base for the dressing in this light, easy noodle salad.

Kosher salt
½ cup smooth **peanut butter**
1 large boneless, skinless **chicken breast** (about 12 ounces), sliced crosswise ¼ inch thick
¼ cup **rice vinegar**
2 tablespoons **soy sauce**
2 tablespoons **Sriracha**, or more as needed
4 **scallions**, thinly sliced (white and green parts)
6 ounces thin **rice noodles** (vermicelli)
1 **romaine heart**, thinly sliced (about 3 cups)
2 **Persian cucumbers** or 1 regular cucumber, thinly sliced (about 2 cups)
1 **red bell pepper**, thinly sliced
1 cup loosely packed roughly chopped fresh **cilantro** (from about 1 medium bunch)
Lime wedges, for serving

START THE WATER: Bring a large pot of salted water to a boil.

POACH THE CHICKEN: Bring 1½ cups water to a simmer in a medium skillet. Whisk in the peanut butter, then add the chicken. Cook over medium-low heat at a bare simmer until just cooked through, 3 to 5 minutes. Use a slotted spoon to transfer the chicken to a plate; continue to simmer the sauce until thickened and reduced by about half, about 5 minutes. Take off the heat and whisk in the vinegar, soy sauce, Sriracha, and scallions. Cool slightly.

COOK THE NOODLES: Add the rice noodles to the boiling water and cook until almost tender, about 3 minutes. Drain and rinse under cold

(continued)

water to cool. Drain the noodles very well, tossing with tongs to release as much water as possible. Snip the noodles with scissors a few times to cut the long strands.

TOSS THE SALAD: Toss the noodles with the romaine, cucumbers, bell pepper, half of the cilantro, and just enough dressing to coat. Season with salt. Divide among 4 bowls and top with the chicken. Drizzle the remaining dressing over the top and garnish with the remaining cilantro. Serve with lime wedges.

Convert this salad into an **ASIAN-STYLE** soup topped with greens and fresh veggies. Add 4 cups of **chicken broth** and an extra cup of **water** to the chicken poaching liquid and bring to a simmer before adding the **chicken, red bell pepper, soy sauce,** and **Sriracha** (skip the rice vinegar). Add the cooked **rice noodles** and **scallions** to the soup and serve in bowls topped with the **lettuce, cucumber, cilantro,** and **lime.**

LINGUINE WITH BELL PEPPER MARINARA

Jarred roasted bell peppers and golden sautéed onions turn into a surprising just-this-side-of-sweet sauce that's perfect for pasta (but would also be good with roast chicken, or drizzled over boiled potatoes). Tell the fam to meet you at the table in half an hour.

¼ cup **extra-virgin olive oil**

4 **garlic cloves**, chopped

1 medium **onion**, chopped

Kosher salt and finely ground **black pepper**

3 (12-ounce) jars **roasted red bell peppers**, drained and chopped

1 teaspoon dried **oregano**, crumbled

¾ cup grated **Parmesan**, plus more for serving

1¼ teaspoons **sugar**

1 pound thin **linguini**

Basil leaves, for serving

SAUTÉ THE ONION: Heat the oil in a medium saucepan over medium heat, then add the garlic, onion, 1½ teaspoons salt, and a couple turns of pepper. Cook, stirring occasionally, until golden, about 15 minutes.

START THE WATER: Bring a large pot of salted water to a boil.

MAKE THE MARINARA: Puree the peppers and oregano with the caramelized onion in a blender until very smooth. Then return to the saucepan and bring to a simmer until slightly thickened, about 8 minutes. Stir in the Parmesan and sugar, and season with salt and pepper. Keep the sauce warm while cooking the pasta.

COOK THE PASTA AND TOSS: Add the pasta to the boiling water and cook according to package directions. Drain and toss with the sauce. Divide the pasta among serving bowls and top with Parmesan and basil.

FARFALLE WITH EGGPLANT YOGURT SAUCE

We like how yogurt adds both creaminess and tang to this Greek-inspired pasta. Any leafy herbs work nicely here if you don't have dill, though definitely keep the basil. This is delicious hot, warm, or cold, and packs up beautifully for a picnic.

1 large **eggplant** (about 1¼ pounds), cut into ½-inch pieces
⅓ cup **extra-virgin olive oil**
Kosher salt and freshly ground **black pepper**
2 cups **cherry tomatoes**, quartered
1 **anchovy fillet**
1 **garlic clove**
1 cup plain **Greek yogurt**
¼ cup chopped fresh **dill**
1 pound **farfalle**
¼ cup torn fresh **basil leaves**

SET UP: Preheat the oven to 450°F.

ROAST THE VEGETABLES: Toss the eggplant with the oil, ½ teaspoon salt, and a couple turns of pepper on a rimmed baking sheet. Roast, stirring occasionally, until browned and tender, about 25 minutes. Add the tomatoes and continue to roast until the tomatoes are wilted, 5 to 10 minutes more.

START THE WATER: While the vegetables are roasting, bring a large pot of salted water to a boil.

SEASON THE YOGURT: Mash the anchovy and garlic to a paste with ½ teaspoon salt and transfer to a large bowl. Whisk in the yogurt, dill, and a couple turns of pepper.

COOK THE PASTA AND TOSS: Add the pasta to the boiling water and cook according to package directions. Reserve 1½ cups of the pasta cooking water, then drain the pasta. Add the pasta along with 1 cup of the cooking water to the yogurt sauce and toss to combine. Thin with more cooking water until everything is evenly coated. Season with salt and pepper. Serve topped with the roasted vegetables and basil.

CHICKENS
GONE WILD

We (along with almost everyone we know) have an insatiable appetite for chicken: Its versatility and deliciousness make it a constant standby on the air, in our magazine, and on our website. It has appeared on *Chopped* more than a few times, too. Tip to tail, inside and out, every part of the bird has been paired with anything you can imagine. Here's our take with a few new twists on America's favorite meat.

SAUTÉED CHICKEN WITH QUICK MOLE
SAUCE AND CILANTRO RICE

GREEK-SPICED WINGS AND POTATOES
WITH YOGURT DIPPING SAUCE

SPINACH AND CHEESE STUFFED CHICKEN
BREASTS WITH HERBED NUTS

SAUCY MOROCCAN CHICKEN AND LEMON
WITH DATE COUSCOUS

SINGAPORE CHICKEN FRIED RICE

MARKET BASKET: CHICKEN

GRILLED CHICKEN SANDWICH
WITH PARSLEY PESTO

JERK CHICKEN, SAUSAGE,
AND CELERY FRICASSEE

ROASTED CHICKEN PROVENÇAL

GRILLED CHICKEN WITH
PEACH PICKLE BBQ SAUCE

GRILLED CHICKEN TONNATO WITH
ARUGULA SALAD

Cooking rice in pureed **CILANTRO** infuses each grain with flavor. Use this technique with other leafy herbs, like parsley or dill.

SAUTÉED CHICKEN
WITH QUICK MOLE SAUCE AND CILANTRO RICE

This incredibly flavorful mole uses nontraditional ingredients (like nut butter, soy sauce, and Chinese five-spice) to cut prep time by hours. Using ancho chile powder instead of a blend gives the dish a clean and round flavor that doesn't fight with the five-spice.

1½ cups loosely packed fresh **cilantro**

3 tablespoons **vegetable oil**

1¼ cups medium-grain **white rice**

Kosher salt and freshly ground **black pepper**

4 small boneless, skinless **chicken breasts**
   (6 to 8 ounces each)

1 teaspoon **Chinese five-spice powder**

1½ tablespoons **chile powder**, preferably ancho

1 **garlic clove**, minced

1½ tablespoons **peanut** or **almond butter**

2 teaspoons **soy sauce**

2 teaspoons **sugar**

1 teaspoon **cocoa powder**

COOK THE RICE: Puree 1 cup of the cilantro with 1¾ cups water in a blender. Heat 1 tablespoon of the oil in a medium saucepan over medium-high heat. Add the rice and cook, stirring, until opaque, about 1 minute. Add the cilantro water and ½ teaspoon salt and bring to a boil. Cover, reduce the heat to low, and cook undisturbed until the rice is tender and absorbs all the liquid, about 18 minutes. Let stand, covered, until ready to serve. Fluff with a fork and stir in the remaining ½ cup cilantro before serving.

SAUTÉ THE CHICKEN: Sprinkle the chicken with ½ teaspoon of the five-spice, ¾ teaspoon salt, and a couple turns of pepper. Heat a large skillet over medium-high heat and pour in 1 tablespoon of the oil. Add

(continued)

the chicken and cook, flipping once, until golden brown on both sides and partially cooked through, 6 minutes per side. Transfer the chicken to a plate.

START THE MOLE: Heat the remaining 1 tablespoon oil in the skillet over medium heat. Add the chile powder, garlic, and remaining ½ teaspoon five-spice and cook, stirring, for 30 seconds. Add ½ cup water and stir to combine. Add the nut butter, soy sauce, sugar, and cocoa powder and whisk until combined. Add 1 more cup water and bring to a simmer.

FINISH AND SERVE: Add the chicken to the sauce and simmer the chicken, flipping occasionally, until it is cooked through and the sauce has thickened, about 12 minutes. Serve the chicken and mole sauce with the cilantro rice on the side.

You'll usually find toasted or dark **SESAME OIL** in the Asian aisle of your grocery store, but sesame's a common seasoning throughout the Mediterranean, Middle East, and Mexico, too. A splash of it adds nutty warmth to sauces and marinades, salads and slaws. Keep it in the fridge.

GREEK-SPICED WINGS AND **POTATOES** WITH YOGURT DIPPING SAUCE

Want ultra-crisp chicken and potatoes? Preheat a roasting pan to jump-start the process. Whip up the sauce while they roast.

3 tablespoons **extra-virgin olive oil**

2 teaspoons dried **oregano**

1 teaspoon grated **lemon zest**

2 **garlic cloves**, finely grated

Kosher salt and freshly ground **black pepper**

3½ pounds split **chicken wings**, tips removed

2 medium **russet potatoes**, cut in ½-inch-thick wedges

1 medium **cucumber**

1 cup plain **Greek yogurt**

1 tablespoon fresh **lemon juice** (about ½ lemon)

¾ teaspoon **toasted sesame oil**

2 tablespoons chopped fresh **dill**

Lemon wedges, for serving

SET UP: Preheat the oven to 425°F with racks in the lower and upper thirds. Put a baking sheet on each rack and preheat for 10 minutes.

ROAST THE CHICKEN AND POTATOES: Combine the olive oil, oregano, lemon zest, garlic, 1¼ teaspoons salt, and a couple turns of pepper in a large bowl. Add the wings and potatoes and toss to coat. Divide them evenly between the hot baking sheets. Return to the oven and bake without stirring until the potatoes and chicken are deep golden brown, crisp, and cooked through, 35 to 40 minutes.

STIR THE SAUCE TOGETHER: Peel the cucumber and halve it lengthwise. Use a spoon to scrape out the seeds, then coarsely grate the cucumber. Stir the cucumber into the yogurt along with the lemon juice, sesame oil, and dill. Season with salt and pepper.

SERVE: Put the wings and potatoes on plates and serve with the lemon wedges and the yogurt sauce for dipping.

SPINACH AND CHEESE STUFFED CHICKEN BREASTS WITH HERBED NUTS

Bone-in, skin-on breasts are perfect for stuffing and roasting, as they stay tender throughout the process. This almost all-pantry dish uses walnuts twice: to bind the stuffing and to add a final crunch at the end.

¾ cup **walnuts**

10 ounces frozen **spinach**, thawed and squeezed very dry

1 cup shredded **mozzarella** (about 4 ounces)

½ cup shredded sharp **Cheddar** (about 2 ounces)

1 tablespoon fresh **lemon juice** (about ½ lemon)

1 teaspoon chopped fresh **thyme**

3 tablespoons chopped fresh **flat-leaf parsley leaves**

Kosher salt and freshly ground **black pepper**

4 (8-ounce) bone-in, skin-on **chicken breasts**

1 tablespoon **extra-virgin olive oil**

SET UP: Preheat the oven to 375°F.

PREP THE FILLING: Spread the nuts on a baking sheet and toast them until light golden and fragrant, about 4 minutes. Let cool, then pulse ½ cup of the nuts in a food processor until finely ground. Add the spinach and pulse until finely chopped. Add the mozzarella, Cheddar, lemon juice, thyme, 2 tablespoons of the parsley, ½ teaspoon salt, and a couple turns of pepper, and pulse just to combine.

STUFF THE CHICKEN: Form the spinach filling into 4 dense ovals. Cut a deep 3-inch-wide pocket lengthwise into the thickest part of each breast with a paring knife. Stuff the breasts with the spinach (they will be very full). Sprinkle the chicken all over with ½ teaspoon salt and a couple turns of pepper.

ROAST THE CHICKEN: Heat a large ovenproof skillet over medium-high heat. When hot, pour in the oil. Cook the chicken skin-side down until golden brown, 4 to 6 minutes. Flip the chicken and transfer the skillet to the oven. Bake until the chicken is cooked through (an instant-read thermometer inserted into the filling should register 160°F), about 30 minutes.

GARNISH AND SERVE: Chop the remaining ¼ cup nuts and stir them together with the remaining 1 tablespoon parsley. Sprinkle the nut mixture over the chicken breasts and serve.

We loved this nutty, cheesy spinach combination in a twice-baked potato; it's a great side dish that's also filling enough to be dinner alone. Slit 4 baked russet potatoes down the center and scoop out most of the potato flesh. Mash with all of the filling ingredients, plus ¼ cup olive oil, salt, and pepper. Re-stuff the potatoes, top with additional Cheddar, and bake until the cheese has melted. Serve with a dollop of sour cream.

POTATO -IZE IT

Q:
WHAT IS YOUR
MOST OFF-
THE-BEATEN-
PATH PANTRY
INGREDIENT?

A:
"I love preserved
lemons."

—JUDGE GEOFFREY
ZAKARIAN

SAUCY MOROCCAN CHICKEN AND LEMON WITH DATE COUSCOUS

Preserved lemons—lemons that have been salt-cured or sun-pickled for weeks—are a classic ingredient in Middle Eastern cooking. Here, salting and sugaring sliced lemons and letting them stand for ten minutes gets you a similar flavor without the wait or the shopping trip. Once they've been salted, caramelized, and stewed, try a bite—they're ultra-flavorful and provide a refreshing counterpoint to the hearty chicken stew.

1 **lemon**, cut into ¼-inch rounds (ends and seeds discarded)

2 teaspoons **sugar**

Kosher salt and freshly ground **black pepper**

½ teaspoon ground **cinnamon**

½ teaspoon ground **coriander**

8 small boneless, skinless **chicken thighs** (about 2 pounds)

3 tablespoons **extra-virgin olive oil**

1½ cups **couscous**

¼ cup chopped pitted **dates** or **golden raisins**

½ cup loosely packed chopped fresh **cilantro**

3 tablespoons **tomato paste**

1 (15-ounce) can **chickpeas**, rinsed and drained

SEASON THE LEMONS: Sprinkle both sides of the lemon slices with the sugar, ¼ teaspoon salt, and a couple turns of pepper. Arrange on a plate and let stand 10 minutes.

BROWN THE CHICKEN: Heat a large skillet over medium-high heat. Combine the cinnamon, coriander, 1 teaspoon salt, and a couple turns of pepper. Sprinkle over the chicken. Put 1 tablespoon of the oil in the skillet. Add the chicken and cook, turning once, until the chicken is golden brown on both sides (but not cooked through), about 3 minutes per side. Transfer to a plate.

(continued)

MAKE THE COUSCOUS: Bring 2 cups water to a boil in a medium saucepan with 1 tablespoon of the oil and a pinch of salt; add the couscous and dates. Cover, remove from the heat, and set aside until tender, about 10 minutes. Fluff with a fork and stir in half of the cilantro just before serving.

CARAMELIZE THE LEMONS: Add the remaining 1 tablespoon oil to the skillet and reduce the heat to medium. Add the lemon slices in a single layer and cook until golden brown and caramelized on both sides, about 3 minutes total. Transfer to the plate with the chicken.

FINISH THE SAUCE: Add the tomato paste to the skillet and cook, stirring, until the paste is a shade darker, about 1 minute. Add 1½ cups water, the chickpeas, chicken, and lemon slices and simmer, flipping the chicken occasionally, until the chicken is just cooked through, about 12 minutes. Stir in the remaining cilantro and serve on top of the couscous.

SINGAPORE CHICKEN FRIED RICE

Curry powder and fish sauce combine forces to turn leftover rice into a brightly seasoned stir-fry.

1 pound boneless, skinless **chicken thighs**, cut into ¾-inch pieces

1 tablespoon **soy sauce**

2 tablespoons **cornstarch**

3 tablespoons **vegetable oil**

2 large **eggs**, lightly beaten

1 (1-inch) piece fresh **ginger**, peeled and minced

2 **garlic cloves**, thinly sliced

1 bunch **scallions**, chopped (white and green parts kept separate)

1 tablespoon **curry powder**

3 cups **cooked rice**

3 plum **tomatoes**, chopped

2 tablespoons **Asian fish sauce**

Kosher salt

COAT THE CHICKEN: Toss the chicken in a bowl in the soy sauce, then coat thoroughly with the cornstarch.

COOK THE EGGS: Heat a wok or large nonstick skillet over medium-high heat until very hot. Pour in 1 tablespoon of the oil. Add the eggs and swirl to spread evenly and form a thin omelet. Cook until set, about 2 minutes. Remove from the heat, fold the omelet in half, and transfer to a cutting board; cut into strips.

BROWN THE CHICKEN: Return the wok to the heat and add the remaining 2 tablespoons oil. When hot, add the chicken, ginger, garlic, scallion whites, and curry powder, and stir-fry until the chicken is well browned on all sides and almost cooked through, about 6 minutes.

TOSS THE RICE: Add the rice and cook, stirring often, until hot, about 2 minutes. Add the tomatoes, fish sauce, and scallion greens and continue to cook until the chicken is cooked through and the tomatoes just start to break down, about 1 minute more. Stir in the egg, season with salt, and serve.

CRISP, TART APPLES

MARKET BASKET

Depending on what's in your fridge, a weeknight dinner can very quickly start to resemble an episode of *Chopped*. We asked our chefs what they would do with a basket of random-seeming everyday ingredients, plus pantry staples. The results might surprise you.

EACH RECIPE SERVES 4

ALMOND BUTTER

KALE

SMALL BONELESS, SKINLESS CHICKEN BREASTS

GRILLED CHICKEN BANH MI WITH ALMOND MAYO AND PICKLED APPLE KALE SLAW

Warm 3 tablespoons each **rice vinegar** and **Asian fish sauce.** Pour over 1 **apple** and 1 **carrot** cut into matchsticks. Stir in 1½ cups stemmed and thinly sliced **kale** and let stand for 15 minutes. Mix ⅓ cup each **almond butter** and **mayonnaise** with 2 tablespoons **Sriracha.** Coat 4 **chicken breasts** in 1 tablespoon **vegetable oil,** 1 teaspoon **soy sauce,** and ½ teaspoon **kosher salt.** Grill on a medium-high grill until cooked through, 8 to 10 minutes per side. Let rest 5 minutes, then slice. Spread the almond mayo on both sides of 4 warmed **hero rolls.** Fill with chicken slices and top with the pickled apple slaw and 2 tablespoons each of torn fresh **basil** and **mint leaves.** TOTAL TIME: 40 MINUTES

ALMOND FRIED CHICKEN WITH ROASTED KALE AND APPLES

Chop the leaves from 1 large bunch of **kale** into 2- to 3-inch pieces. Toss on a baking sheet with 2 **apples** cut into thin wedges, 3 tablespoons **vegetable oil,** and ¾ teaspoon **kosher salt.** Bake at 425°F, stirring occasionally, until the apples are tender and the kale is crisp, about 20 minutes. Whisk ½ cup **almond butter** with ⅓ cup **milk,** 1 tablespoon **honey,** and 1 teaspoon kosher salt. Dredge 4 **chicken breasts** in **all-purpose flour,** coat with the almond butter mixture, then roll in 2 cups **panko bread crumbs.** Heat ½ inch vegetable oil in a large skillet over medium-high heat to 350°F. Panfry the chicken, adjusting the heat as necessary to keep from burning, until crispy and cooked through, 5 to 6 minutes per side. Serve with the roasted kale and apple and a squeeze of **lemon.** TOTAL TIME: 50 MINUTES

SPICY AFRICAN CHICKEN AND ALMOND STEW

Cut 4 **chicken breasts** into 1-inch chunks and sprinkle with 1 teaspoon **kosher salt** and a couple turns of **pepper.** Heat a Dutch oven over medium-high heat. When hot, pour in 2 tablespoons **vegetable oil.** Add the chicken and cook, turning often, until brown on all sides, about 6 minutes; transfer to a bowl. Add another tablespoon of vegetable oil to the pan and reduce the heat to medium. Add 1 cup chopped **onion,** 1 tablespoon each minced fresh **garlic** and **ginger,** and 1 teaspoon kosher salt. Cook until softened, about 5 minutes. Add 1 **sweet potato** and 1 **apple** cut into 1-inch chunks, ¾ teaspoon **cayenne,** and 3 cups each **chicken broth** and **water,** and bring to a simmer. Add 6 cups stemmed and chopped **kale,** 1 large chopped **tomato,** and ½ cup **almond butter.** Stir to combine and simmer until the vegetables are tender, 10 to 15 minutes. Return the chicken to the pot and simmer until just cooked through, about 5 minutes. Serve with ½ cup **cilantro leaves** scattered over the top. TOTAL TIME: 50 MINUTES

GRILLED CHICKEN SANDWICH
WITH **PARSLEY PESTO**

Parsley pesto adds brightness to a simple weeknight dinner sandwich. It can be made with any nut—we especially like it with pecans—so feel free to swap in whatever you have in your pantry.

¼ cup coarsely chopped **pecans, almonds, or walnuts**

2 cups fresh **flat-leaf parsley leaves** (from 1 large bunch)

½ small **garlic clove**

Kosher salt and freshly ground **black pepper**

¼ cup plus 1 tablespoon grated **Parmesan**

¼ cup plus 1 tablespoon **extra-virgin olive oil**

1 to 2 teaspoons fresh **lemon juice**, to taste

4 **hamburger buns**

1 large **egg white**, lightly beaten

1 teaspoon crushed **red pepper flakes**

1 teaspoon **fennel seeds**, lightly crushed

2 large boneless, skinless **chicken breasts** (10 to 12 ounces each)

1 large **tomato**, sliced

SET UP: Preheat the oven to 375°F.

MAKE THE PESTO: Pulse the nuts in a food processor until finely ground. Add the parsley, garlic, ¼ teaspoon salt, and a couple turns of pepper, and pulse until finely chopped. Add the ¼ cup Parmesan and pulse to combine. With the motor running, drizzle in the ¼ cup oil and blend until combined. Transfer to a bowl and stir in the lemon juice.

TOAST THE BUNS: Brush the tops of the hamburger buns with egg white. Sprinkle the tops with the remaining 1 tablespoon Parmesan, half of the red pepper flakes, and half of the fennel seeds. Bake until lightly toasted and set, about 6 minutes.

GRILL THE CHICKEN: Prepare a grill or grill pan and heat to medium-high heat. Halve the chicken breasts crosswise and pound each piece to a thickness of about ¾ inch. Toss them with the remaining 1 tablespoon

oil, ¾ teaspoon salt, and the remaining red pepper flakes and fennel seeds. Grill the chicken, flipping once, until just cooked through, about 8 minutes total.

BUILD THE SANDWICHES: Sandwich the grilled chicken on the buns with the pesto and tomato slices.

JERK CHICKEN, SAUSAGE, AND CELERY FRICASSEE

Jerk seasoning (a combo of allspice, thyme, and hot pepper) and spicy andouille sausage bring the heat to this flavorful chicken skillet. Use the inner stalks of celery here—they cook quickly and end up melting into the sauce.

2 ounces **andouille sausage**, finely chopped (about ½ cup)

1 tablespoon **extra-virgin olive oil**

4 **chicken legs** (thighs and drumsticks, about 2½ pounds)

Kosher salt and freshly ground **pepper** (preferably white)

1 tablespoon **all-purpose flour**

3 **scallions**, chopped (white and green parts kept separate)

2 **garlic cloves**, minced

1 tablespoon minced **jalapeño**, seeded if desired

¼ teaspoon ground **allspice**

1 large sprig of fresh **thyme**

6 **celery stalks**, preferably from the heart, cut into 3-inch pieces

RENDER THE SAUSAGE: Put the sausage and olive oil in a large, cold nonstick skillet and cook over medium heat until the fat starts to render and the sausage starts to brown, about 6 minutes. Transfer the sausage to a small plate with a slotted spoon.

BROWN THE CHICKEN: Sprinkle the chicken with ¾ teaspoon salt and a couple turns of pepper, then toss in the flour to coat. Increase the heat under the skillet to medium-high and sear the chicken, skin-side down, until golden brown, about 8 minutes.

FINISH THE FRICASSEE: Flip the chicken skin-side up. Add ¾ cup water, the sausage, scallion whites, garlic, jalapeño, allspice, and thyme. Arrange the celery around the chicken and bring to a simmer. Reduce the heat to medium-low, cover, and cook until the chicken is cooked through and the celery is crisp-tender, 20 to 25 minutes. Serve topped with the scallion greens.

ROASTED CHICKEN PROVENÇAL

Sunny Provençal vegetables and orange marmalade melt into a sweet-and-sour sauce with a salty, savory punch of olives and anchovies. This goes great with Cauliflower and Cannellini Bean Mash (page 124) or Buttery Roasted Potatoes with Wilted Spinach (page 132).

3 medium **tomatoes**, cut into 1-inch wedges
1 large **onion**, cut into 1-inch-thick wedges
1 red or yellow **bell pepper**, cut into 1-inch-thick strips
¼ cup pitted **Niçoise** or **kalamata olives**
4 **anchovy fillets**, coarsely chopped
2 tablespoons **orange marmalade**
1 tablespoon **extra-virgin olive oil**
Kosher salt
1 (3- to 4-pound) **whole chicken**
1 small sprig of fresh **rosemary**
Freshly ground **black pepper**

SET UP: Preheat the oven to 425°F.

TOSS THE VEGETABLES: Scatter the tomatoes, onion, bell pepper, olives, anchovies, marmalade, and oil in a large roasting pan. Add 1 tablespoon water and ¼ teaspoon salt and toss to coat thoroughly.

PREP THE CHICKEN: Pat the chicken dry, insert the rosemary into its cavity, and sprinkle with 1½ teaspoons salt and a couple turns of pepper. Push the vegetables to the sides of the roasting pan and put the chicken breast-side up in the center.

ROAST THE CHICKEN AND SERVE: Transfer the chicken to the oven and cook for 30 minutes. Flip the chicken so that it is breast-side down and continue to roast until golden brown all over, about 15 minutes. Flip the chicken back to breast-side up and continue to roast until the vegetables are saucy and tender and the chicken is cooked through (an instant-read thermometer inserted into the thigh should register 165°F), about 15 minutes more. Let rest for 10 minutes, then cut the chicken into pieces and serve with the vegetables.

SERVES 2 TO 4

ACTIVE TIME

25 minutes

TOTAL TIME

1 hour

When blending **HOT LIQUIDS,** let the liquid cool for 5 minutes or so before transferring to a blender, filling only halfway. Put the lid on but leave one corner open; this will prevent the vacuum effect that creates heat explosions. Cover the lid with a kitchen towel to catch splatters and carefully pulse until smooth.

GRILLED CHICKEN WITH PEACH PICKLE BBQ SAUCE

Peach preserves and dill pickles are the backbone of this sweet-tangy barbecue sauce. Grilling big pieces of chicken (or any cut of meat) over gentle indirect heat ensures the inside gets perfectly cooked before the outside has a chance to burn.

2 tablespoons **vegetable oil**, plus more for the grill
2 **chicken halves** (4 to 5 pounds total)
Kosher salt and freshly ground **black pepper**
½ medium **onion**, chopped
1 tablespoon **chile powder**
¼ cup **ketchup**
3 tablespoons **peach preserves**
¼ cup chopped **dill pickles**

SET UP: Prepare an outdoor grill so that you have a medium-hot fire for both direct and indirect grilling (move hot coals to just one side of the grill, or turn on only half the burners on a gas grill). Once hot, brush the grill grates with oil.

GRILL THE CHICKEN: Pat the chicken dry and sprinkle with 1 teaspoon salt and a couple turns of pepper. Grill the chicken, skin-side up, over direct heat (the hotter side) until lightly charred, about 4 minutes. Flip and cook until faint grill marks appear on the skin, 3 to 5 minutes more. Flip again and move the chicken to the indirect side of the grill (the cooler side). Cover and cook until an instant-read thermometer inserted into the thigh registers 165°F, about 40 minutes.

MAKE THE BBQ SAUCE: Meanwhile, heat the 2 tablespoons oil in a medium saucepan over medium-high heat. Add the onion and cook, stirring occasionally, until softened, about 8 minutes. Add the chile powder and cook, stirring, for about 1 minute. Add the ketchup, peach preserves, and ½ cup water and bring to a simmer. Simmer until slightly thickened, about 8 minutes. Add the pickles. Puree with an immersion blender or transfer to a blender. Set aside 1 cup of the sauce for serving.

BASTE AND SERVE: When the chicken is just fully cooked, begin basting it with some of the remaining BBQ sauce and move it back to direct heat. Continue to baste it, gently flipping often, until glazed and lightly charred, about 5 minutes. Serve with the reserved BBQ sauce on the side.

Even when you buy
cutlets that have
been pounded, they
can be uneven, so
we pound them a
little more with a
small skillet or **MEAT
MALLET** to make
them super-thin and
even.

GRILLED CHICKEN TONNATO
WITH ARUGULA SALAD

Red peppers add brightness to tonnato sauce (a classic Italian
condiment made with mayonnaise and tuna, usually served with
veal), which does double duty here as a topping for chicken cutlets
pounded extra thin and as a salad dressing; it's great with the lemony
arugula.

1 **red bell pepper**, diced

3 tablespoons fresh **lemon juice** (1 to 1½ lemons)

1 tablespoon drained brined **capers**

5 to 7 ounces canned **tuna** packed in olive oil, drained

½ cup **mayonnaise**

3 tablespoons **extra-virgin olive oil**

Kosher salt and freshly ground **black pepper**

4 **chicken cutlets** (about 1½ pounds)

6 cups **baby arugula**

2 cups **grape tomatoes**, halved

½ cup loosely packed fresh **basil leaves**,
   roughly chopped

2 tablespoons chopped pitted **green olives**

SET UP: Prepare a grill or grill pan and heat to medium-high heat.

BLEND THE SAUCE: Puree a third of the bell pepper, the lemon juice,
and capers in a blender until almost smooth. Add the tuna, mayonnaise,
and 2 tablespoons of the oil and blend until smooth, about 1 minute.
Season with salt and pepper.

POUND THE CUTLETS: Working with one at a time, put a cutlet
between two pieces of plastic wrap and pound with a small skillet or
meat mallet until evenly flattened to about ¼ inch (it's OK if the cutlets
break a little bit).

GRILL THE CUTLETS: Coat the cutlets with the remaining tablespoon oil and sprinkle with ¾ teaspoon salt and a couple turns of pepper. Grill on one side until almost cooked through, 2 to 3 minutes. Flip and continue to grill until just cooked through, about 1 minute more.

TOSS AND SERVE: Toss together the arugula, the remaining bell pepper, the tomatoes, basil, and olives with just enough of the tonnato sauce to coat. Serve the chicken topped with the salad and drizzled with more tonnato sauce. (You may have a little sauce left over; extra sauce keeps for up to 3 days refrigerated.)

Everything is more fun in a pita and the tonnato sauce is especially good on falafel. Fry or bake up a batch of your favorite falafel and toss it with the salad ingredients, enough tonnato sauce to coat, and some sliced hard-boiled egg. Then tuck it all into a pita pocket and drizzle with more tonnato sauce and a couple dashes of hot sauce. Roasted cauliflower also works nicely in place of falafel.

PUT IT
IN YOUR
POCKET

EGGS

AFTER BREAKFAST

This chapter is actually part of our campaign to elevate eggs from their humble breakfast station to their rightful place as kings of any meal. They are pre-portioned, good-looking, great-tasting, and lightning fast to cook. Really, what isn't better with an egg in—or on—it?

PIZZA STRATA

SKILLET SPAGHETTI CASSEROLE

MEAT AND POTATOES QUICHE

SWISS CHARD BAKED EGGS

CHEDDAR KALE SOUFFLÉ

HAVE FUN WITH YOUR FRITTATA

PHILLY-STYLE GARLICKY GREENS
AND EGG SANDWICH

EGGS POACHED IN MARTINI MARINARA

NACHO BAKE

PROSCIUTTO-PESTO CODDLED EGG CUPS

DAY-OLD BREAD
soaks up sauce without getting soggy. If you only have fresh, toast the cubes in a low oven to dry them out a bit.

PIZZA STRATA

Strata is another name for a savory bread pudding. Here you get all the flavors of deep-dish pizza in an easy-to-make (and easy-to-make-ahead) casserole that tastes just as good the next day. (A couple of us found this in our refrigerator the day after testing and devoured the entire thing for lunch.)

2 tablespoons **extra-virgin olive oil**, plus more for the dish

3 **garlic cloves**, finely chopped

1 (28-ounce) can diced **tomatoes**

1½ teaspoons dried **oregano**

Kosher salt and freshly ground **black pepper**

4 large **eggs**

1 cup **half-and-half**

8 cups cubed stale **Italian bread** (about a 12-ounce loaf)

2 ounces sliced **pepperoni** (about ¼ cup)

1½ cups shredded **mozzarella** (about 6 ounces)

SET UP: Preheat the oven to 400°F. Oil a 2-quart baking dish.

SIMMER THE SAUCE: Heat the oil in a medium saucepan over medium heat until hot, then add the garlic and swirl until golden, about 2 minutes. Stir in the tomatoes with their juice, the oregano, ¾ teaspoon salt, and a couple turns of pepper and simmer until thickened, about 8 minutes. Remove from the heat and cool to warm.

MAKE THE CUSTARD: Beat the eggs with the half-and-half and ½ teaspoon salt and a couple turns of pepper. Beat into the cooled tomato sauce and transfer to the prepared baking dish.

ASSEMBLE AND BAKE: Toss the bread and pepperoni in the tomato-egg sauce. Sprinkle with the cheese. Bake the strata until the custard is set, 35 to 40 minutes.

You can use 4 cups of **LEFTOVER SPAGHETTI** instead of starting with dry; just skip the part where you cook the pasta and go straight to tossing it with the capers, raisins, red pepper flakes, and butter.

SKILLET SPAGHETTI CASSEROLE

Spaghetti meets its match in this sweet-salty casserole. Raisins might sound crazy here, but alongside briny capers and spicy pepper flakes, they round out the flavors and add pops of bright sweetness. If you don't have raisins, other dried fruit would work—just cut into raisin-size bits before adding.

Kosher salt
8 ounces **spaghetti**
¼ cup drained brined **capers**
¼ cup **golden raisins**
¼ teaspoon crushed **red pepper flakes**
4 tablespoons (½ stick) **unsalted butter**
8 large **eggs**
2 tablespoons **extra-virgin olive oil**
Freshly ground **black pepper**
½ cup grated **Parmesan**
8 ounces shredded **mozzarella** (2 cups)

SET UP: Preheat the broiler to high with a rack set 6 inches from the heat source. Bring a large pot of salted water to a boil.

BOIL THE PASTA: Add the pasta to the water and cook according to package directions. Drain and immediately return to the pot. Toss the pasta with the capers, raisins, red pepper flakes, and 3 tablespoons of the butter until the pasta is well coated.

COOK THE CASSEROLE: Beat the eggs with the oil, 1 teaspoon salt, and a couple turns of black pepper in a medium bowl. Heat the remaining tablespoon butter in a large ovenproof nonstick skillet over medium heat. Add the beaten eggs and cook, without stirring, until just set on the bottom, about 30 seconds. Then lift some of the set eggs with a spatula, letting the uncooked egg flow down to the bottom of the skillet. Repeat until the eggs are mostly set but still runny. Nestle the pasta evenly into the eggs and scatter the cheeses over the top. Broil, watching carefully, until the cheese is melted and the eggs are fully set, about 3 minutes. Cut into wedges and serve.

Baking the **PIE CRUST** before adding the filling helps it stay crisp. If you don't own pie weights, dried beans or uncooked rice will do the trick.

MEAT AND POTATOES QUICHE

Leftover mashed potatoes turn quiche into a hearty dinner. Round this out with an assertive salad—we like it with frisée or escarole; see Vinaigrettes (page 165).

1 sheet refrigerated **pie dough** (from a 14-ounce package)
1 pound bulk sweet or hot **Italian sausage**
6 slices **bacon**, chopped
1 cup leftover **mashed potatoes**
6 large **eggs**
1½ cups **half-and-half**
Kosher salt and freshly ground **black pepper**

SET UP: Preheat the oven to 400°F.

BLIND-BAKE THE CRUST: Put the dough in a pie plate, crimp the edges, and line with foil. Pour pie weights on top and bake until the crust sets, about 20 minutes. Remove the foil with the weights and continue to bake the crust until golden, about 15 minutes more. Remove the crust from the oven and let cool. Reduce the oven temperature to 375°F.

COOK THE SAUSAGE: Meanwhile, put the sausage and bacon in a cold large skillet over medium heat and cook, breaking up the sausage lumps with a wooden spoon, until browned, about 10 minutes. Drain off the fat.

ASSEMBLE AND BAKE: Spread the potatoes evenly over the bottom of the crust. Top with the sausage and bacon. Beat the eggs with the half-and-half and ½ teaspoon salt and a couple turns of pepper, then pour over the meat. Bake until the quiche is just set, 35 to 40 minutes. Serve warm or at room temperature.

SWISS CHARD BAKED EGGS

The unexpected trio of bracing Swiss chard, rich eggs, and tangy yogurt combines to create the perfect comfort food. This would also be great with toasted pita bread on the side for scooping.

Unsalted butter, for the dish

2 large bunches of **Swiss chard**

¼ cup **extra-virgin olive oil**

1 large **shallot**, sliced

Kosher salt and finely ground **black pepper**

6 large **eggs**

½ cup **Greek yogurt**

1 teaspoon fresh **lime juice** (about ½ lime)

¼ teaspoon crushed **red pepper flakes**

Crusty bread, for serving

SET UP: Preheat the oven to 400°F. Butter a 3-quart baking dish.

SAUTÉ THE GREENS: Remove the stems from the chard leaves and chop the stems. Heat the oil in a large skillet over medium heat and sauté the stems with the shallot, 1 teaspoon salt, and a couple turns of black pepper until the shallot is golden, about 8 minutes. Stir in the chard leaves and cook, turning with tongs, until the leaves are wilted, about 4 minutes.

COOK THE EGGS: Transfer the chard to the prepared baking dish and make 6 shallow wells in the leaves. Crack an egg into each and sprinkle the eggs with salt and black pepper. Bake, rotating the dish as needed for even cooking, until the egg whites are set but the yolks are still runny, 10 to 12 minutes.

GARNISH AND SERVE: Stir together the yogurt and lime juice, and season with salt and black pepper to taste. Top the eggs with dollops of the yogurt and sprinkle with the red pepper flakes. Serve the bread on the side.

SERVES 4 TO 6

ACTIVE TIME

20 minutes

TOTAL TIME

1 hour

CHEDDAR KALE SOUFFLÉ

Soufflé may sound advanced, but it's not. The unique thing about this classic, simple egg dish is how it puffs up when the bubbles in the whipped egg whites expand in the oven. It's perfect for a light dinner, brunch, or even part of a holiday breakfast. We use frozen kale here, but if you have other greens in your freezer, swap those in.

Unsalted butter, for the dish

2 tablespoons **extra-virgin olive oil**

1 medium **onion**, chopped

1 (16-ounce) package frozen **kale**, thawed

Kosher salt and freshly ground **black pepper**

1 cup shredded **Cheddar** (about 4 ounces)

6 large **eggs**

1½ cups **half-and-half**

SET UP: Preheat the oven to 350°F. Butter a 2-quart baking dish.

SAUTÉ THE KALE: Heat the oil in a large skillet over medium heat until hot. Stir in the onion and cook, stirring, until golden, 6 to 8 minutes. Stir in the kale, 1 teaspoon salt, and a couple turns of pepper and cook until tender, about 6 minutes. Transfer the kale to the prepared baking dish. Sprinkle with the Cheddar.

ASSEMBLE AND BAKE THE SOUFFLÉ: Separate the egg whites and yolks. Beat the yolks, half-and-half, and ½ teaspoon salt in a large bowl. In a separate bowl, beat the egg whites and ¼ teaspoon salt with an electric mixer until they hold soft peaks, being careful to not overbeat. Then gently fold the whites into the beaten yolks. Pour the egg batter over the kale and bake until the eggs are set and puffed, about 45 minutes. Serve immediately.

HAVE FUN WITH YOUR
FRITTATA

The frittata (a baked Italian-style omelet, kind of like a crustless quiche) is a classic, easy way to turn leftovers into dinner. These are a few of our favorite combos—use the egg base as a starting point to find your new favorite.

1 **PREHEAT** the oven to 400°F. Whisk 10 large **eggs,** ¼ cup **milk,** ¾ teaspoon **kosher salt,** and a couple turns of freshly ground **black pepper** in a large bowl.

2 **THEN** choose one of these combinations:

BROCCOLI AND CHEDDAR

Add 2 cups chopped cooked **broccoli,** 1 cup shredded **Cheddar,** and ¼ teaspoon **cayenne** to the beaten eggs.

LOW COUNTRY SHRIMP

Add ½ teaspoon **seafood seasoning** (such as Old Bay), 2 tablespoons chopped fresh **flat-leaf parsley leaves,** 1 cup chopped cooked **shrimp,** and ½ cup each sautéed **onion, green bell pepper,** and **celery** to the beaten eggs.

SPANISH POTATO CHIP

Add ½ cup chopped **roasted red peppers,** 2 cups **plain salted potato chips,** ½ teaspoon **smoked sweet paprika,** and 3 tablespoons chopped fresh **flat-leaf parsley leaves** to the beaten eggs.

HAM AND PEAS

Add ¾ cup diced **ham,** 1 cup thawed **frozen peas,** and 1 cup grated **Swiss cheese** to the beaten eggs.

3 **HEAT** 1 tablespoon **extra-virgin olive oil** in a medium ovenproof nonstick skillet over medium-high heat. Add the beaten egg mixture and cook until the edges start to set, about 2 minutes. Transfer to the oven and bake until the center is set, 15 to 20 minutes. Let stand for 5 minutes before sliding carefully onto a serving plate and cutting into wedges.

SERVES 4

ACTIVE TIME

20 minutes

TOTAL TIME

25 minutes

PHILLY-STYLE GARLICKY GREENS AND EGG SANDWICH

Eggs fried in hot sauce and blanched-then-sautéed broccoli rabe combine in a hero that's the perfect balance of spicy, garlicky, rich, and green.

Kosher salt

1½ pounds **broccoli rabe**

3 tablespoons **extra-virgin olive oil**

4 **garlic cloves**, finely chopped

Freshly ground **black pepper**

5 to 6 tablespoons **unsalted butter**

4 (9-inch) **hero rolls**, split

8 ounces sliced **provolone**

3 tablespoons **Sriracha**

4 to 8 large **eggs**

2 tablespoons grated **Parmesan**

SET UP: Preheat the broiler to high with a rack set 4 inches from the heat source. Bring a large pot of salted water to a boil.

COOK THE GREENS: Add the broccoli rabe to the water and cook until crisp tender, 3 to 4 minutes, then drain. Heat the oil in a large skillet over medium-high heat until hot. Add the garlic and cook, stirring, until golden, 1 to 2 minutes. Stir in the broccoli rabe, season with salt and pepper, remove from the heat, and keep warm.

TOAST THE ROLLS: Melt 4 tablespoons of the butter in a large skillet. Brush the cut sides of the rolls with some of the melted butter. Broil the rolls, cut-side up, until brown, about 3 minutes. Divide the provolone among the rolls and broil until the cheese melts, about 1 minute. Fill the rolls with broccoli rabe.

FRY THE EGGS AND ASSEMBLE: Heat one more tablespoon butter in the same skillet over medium-high heat until hot. Stir in the Sriracha and simmer for 20 seconds. Working in batches and adding more butter if needed, crack the eggs into the skillet and fry until the whites just

begin to set, about 1 minute. Cover the skillet and cook over low heat until the egg whites are set but the yolks are still runny, 1 to 2 minutes. Put 1 to 2 eggs on each sandwich, sprinkle with Parmesan, and serve.

EGGS turn leftover sauces, stews, or sautéed vegetables into a filling (and almost-new) meal.

EGGS POACHED
IN MARTINI MARINARA

Dinnertime meets cocktail hour in this tangy tomato sauce spiked with olives and gin to balance out the richness of baked egg yolks.

4 **garlic cloves**
2 tablespoons **extra-virgin olive oil**
1 medium **onion**, chopped
4 sprigs of fresh **thyme**
¼ cup **gin**
1 (28-ounce) can whole **tomatoes** in juice
1 cup **pimento-stuffed olives**, sliced
¼ cup **olive brine**
Kosher salt and freshly ground **black pepper**
8 large **eggs**
4 slices toasted **country bread**

MAKE THE SAUCE: Smash 3 of the garlic cloves. Heat the oil in a large skillet over medium-high heat until hot. Add the smashed garlic, onion, and thyme and cook until golden, about 6 minutes. Add the gin and cook until the liquid has reduced by half. Stir in the tomatoes with their juice, the olives, and brine and bring to a simmer. Cook, stirring occasionally while breaking up the tomatoes, until the sauce is slightly thickened, 10 to 15 minutes. Season with ½ teaspoon salt and a couple turns of pepper.

POACH THE EGGS: Make 8 shallow wells in the sauce. Crack an egg into each and sprinkle with salt and pepper. Cover the skillet and simmer until the egg whites are set but the yolks are still runny, about 8 minutes.

SERVE: Rub the toasted bread slices with the remaining garlic clove and serve with the eggs.

NACHO BAKE

This is everything you love about nachos, made hearty enough for dinner. We discovered that standing the chips upright in the egg mixture gets them crispy on top and adds body to the bake below. This is ridiculously delicious, and difficult to stop eating.

1 pound fresh **chorizo sausage**, casings removed

1 medium **onion**, chopped

1 (15-ounce) can **pinto beans**, rinsed and drained

8 large **eggs**

1 cup **heavy cream**

1 cup **sour cream**

Kosher salt and freshly ground **black pepper**

3 cups **tortilla chips** (about 30)

2 cups shredded **Cheddar** (about 8 ounces)

2 tablespoons fresh **cilantro leaves**

Jarred salsa, for serving

SET UP: Preheat the oven to 350°F.

BROWN THE CHORIZO AND ONION: Cook the chorizo until browned in a large nonstick skillet over medium-high heat, about 8 minutes. Transfer to a 3-quart baking dish, leaving the fat in the skillet. Sauté the onion in the pan drippings until golden, about 6 minutes. Stir in the beans, then transfer to the baking dish.

ASSEMBLE AND BAKE: Beat the eggs, heavy cream, and sour cream with ¾ teaspoon salt and a couple turns of pepper. Gently pour the eggs over the meat and beans. Press the chips into the mixture so they stand up. Sprinkle with the Cheddar and bake until the eggs are just set, about 45 minutes. Sprinkle with the cilantro and serve with salsa.

SERVES 6

ACTIVE TIME

10 minutes

TOTAL TIME

20 minutes

Save **BREAD CRUSTS** in the freezer and blitz in the food processor to make bread crumbs to use in the meatballs on page 22.

PROSCIUTTO-PESTO CODDLED EGG CUPS

These super-quick egg cups would work as well for brunch as they do for dinner. Use your favorite pesto or tapenade to give them your own twist.

> Nonstick cooking spray
> 12 slices **prosciutto**
> 12 slices thin **sandwich bread**
> ¼ cup prepared **pesto**
> ¼ cup grated **Parmesan**
> 12 large **eggs**
> Kosher salt and freshly ground **black pepper**

SET UP: Preheat the oven to 400°F. Lightly spray a 12-cup muffin tin with nonstick cooking spray.

LINE THE TIN: Cut the prosciutto in half and overlap 2 pieces in each cup. Cut twelve 2-inch rounds from the bread and set one in each cup, over the prosciutto.

FILL AND BAKE: Divide the pesto and cheese among the cups. Then crack an egg into each and season with salt and pepper. Bake until the egg whites are set but the yolks are still runny, 8 to 12 minutes. Serve.

FLASH
IN THE PAN

If it's quick-cooking, meaty, and meant for a hot pan (or grill), you'll find it here. Chops, cutlets, and sausages are the perfect base for fast dinners for a couple of reasons—first, they're super-easy and just need a flash of direct heat, and second, they take well to many combinations of flavors, so they'll be delicious with whatever you're craving that day.

SALSA-MARINATED SKIRT STEAK SOFT
TACOS WITH REFRIED WHITE BEANS

STRIP STEAK WITH
RED WINE MUSHROOM SAUCE
AND MUSTARD SMASHED POTATOES

BUTTER-BASTED FLAT IRON STEAK WITH
TOMATO BUTTER SAUCE
AND PARSLEY NOODLES

ITALIAN GYROS WITH YOGURT
AND TOMATO

BROILED PAPRIKA FLANK STEAK WITH
TOASTED SPICED NUTS

CUMIN PORK STEAK WITH
GRILLED SAVOY CABBAGE AND APPLES

GO-TO GUIDE: TEN FUN PAN SAUCES

PRETZEL-MUSTARD-CRUSTED PORK
TENDERLOIN SLIDERS

GARLIC AND VINEGAR GLAZED PORK
CHOPS WITH SCALLIONS

QUICK SKILLET KIELBASA
PORK AND BEANS

RAMP UP YOUR POT ROAST

SALSA-MARINATED SKIRT STEAK SOFT TACOS WITH REFRIED WHITE BEANS

Who said refried beans had to be pintos? Cannellini beans—cooked in the same skillet as the salsa-marinated steak—get the twice-cooked treatment, adding nutty creaminess to meaty tacos.

1½ cups jarred **red salsa** (about 12 ounces)

2 **garlic cloves**, smashed

¼ cup **extra-virgin olive oil**

1 tablespoon **Worcestershire sauce**

1 tablespoon fresh **lime juice** (about 2 limes)

1¼ pounds **skirt steak**, trimmed and cut into 3 pieces

12 (6-inch) **flour tortillas**

Kosher salt and freshly ground **black pepper**

2 (15-ounce) cans **cannellini beans**, with liquid

½ cup loosely packed fresh **cilantro leaves**, coarsely chopped

MARINATE THE STEAK: Combine 1 cup of the salsa, the garlic, 2 tablespoons of the oil, the Worcestershire, and lime juice in a resealable plastic bag and add the steak. Shake to evenly disperse and marinate for at least 30 minutes at room temperature or up to 2 hours in the refrigerator.

SET UP: Preheat the oven to 300°F. Wrap the tortillas in aluminum foil and keep warm in the oven.

SEAR THE STEAKS: Heat a large skillet over medium-high heat. Remove the steaks from the bag, allowing the large salsa bits and extra marinade to drip off, and pat with paper towels to dry slightly. Sprinkle with 1 teaspoon salt and a couple turns of pepper. Pour the remaining 2 tablespoons oil into the skillet and cook the steaks on one side until browned, about 4 minutes. Flip and cook until charred and medium-rare, about 3 more minutes. Let rest on a cutting board before slicing.

(continued)

MASH THE BEANS: Add the beans with their liquid to the same skillet and cook until the liquid has reduced by half, 4 to 6 minutes. Mash with a potato masher until smooth.

ASSEMBLE THE TACOS: Slice the steak against the grain into 2- to 3-inch-long pieces. Spread the center of each tortilla with 1 tablespoon of the beans. Arrange a few slices of steak on top of each with some of the remaining salsa and some cilantro. Serve the extra beans on the side.

RAISE THE CHEESE-STEAKS

These steak-filled soft tacos can easily be reworked into satisfying MEXICAN HEROS. Warm the **salsa, Worcestershire,** and **lime juice** in a skillet, then add 12 ounces deli **roast beef** and toss to warm through. Spread the **mashed beans** onto 4 toasted **hoagie rolls,** and mound the meat and salsa inside. Top with a heaping layer of grated **pepper Jack cheese,** and broil until melty. Serve with extra lime and salsa.

Q:

WHAT IS YOUR DREAM *CHOPPED* BASKET?

A:

"My dream *Chopped* basket probably won't ever happen: New York strip steak and potatoes."

—HOST TED ALLEN

STRIP STEAK WITH RED WINE MUSHROOM SAUCE AND MUSTARD SMASHED POTATOES

This is classic meat and potatoes, with a few extra flavor notes. Chicken broth and mustard add richness and zing to milk-free smashed potatoes, while bay leaves bring gentle earthiness to the spice rub for the steaks.

1 large dried **bay leaf**

Kosher salt

2 teaspoons dried **oregano**

½ teaspoon crushed **red pepper flakes**

4 (8-ounce) boneless **strip steaks**, each about 1 inch thick

1½ pounds **russet potatoes**, peeled and cut into ½-inch pieces

6 tablespoons (¾ stick) **unsalted butter**

¾ cup **chicken broth**

1 tablespoon **whole-grain mustard**

3 tablespoons **vegetable oil**

12 ounces **button** or **cremini mushrooms**, quartered

1 cup **red wine**

GRIND THE SPICE MIX: Combine the bay leaf, 1 tablespoon salt, the oregano, and red pepper flakes in a coffee or spice grinder and pulse until finely ground. Rub evenly into the surface of the steaks. Set aside to marinate at room temperature for 15 minutes.

MAKE THE SMASHED POTATOES: Meanwhile, put the potatoes in a heavy-bottomed saucepan with enough cold water to cover by ½ inch. Salt the water generously, bring to a simmer, and cook, covered, until the potatoes are fork tender, about 10 minutes. Drain, return to the pot with 3 tablespoons of the butter, and mash with a fork or potato masher. Stir in ¼ cup of the chicken broth and the mustard until creamy. Season with salt to taste.

SEAR THE STEAKS: Heat a large skillet over medium-high heat. When hot, pour in 2 tablespoons of the oil. Cook 2 of the steaks until crusty and browned on one side, about 5 minutes. Flip and cook until browned on the other side, about 4 minutes more. Remove the steaks and set aside to rest. Wipe out the skillet, add the remaining oil, and repeat with the remaining steaks.

MAKE THE PAN SAUCE: Add the mushrooms to the skillet and cook until browned, about 3 minutes. Add the red wine and the remaining ½ cup chicken broth and cook until reduced by half, about 5 minutes. Swirl in the remaining 3 tablespoons butter until the sauce is glossy and thick.

SERVE: Transfer the steaks to 4 plates and divide the potatoes among the plates. Spoon the sauce over the top and serve.

To get a great crust on **STEAK,** first dry it well with paper towels. Heat a heavy skillet over medium-high heat; add a swirl of oil and/or butter. Season the meat generously with salt and pepper and lay in the pan. Don't move it for the first few minutes; when the crust is brown enough, it'll release from the pan on its own.

BUTTER-BASTED FLAT IRON STEAK WITH TOMATO BUTTER SAUCE AND PARSLEY NOODLES

Basting steaks with hot herb butter speeds up cooking time (by applying heat to both sides of the steak at once) while infusing every bite with flavor. Charring cherry tomatoes intensifies their flavor and softens them into a quick sauce that tastes like it took much longer to make than it did.

Kosher salt

2 tablespoons **vegetable oil**

4 (½-inch-thick) top blade **chuck steaks** (flat iron steaks),
    1½ pounds total

Freshly ground **black pepper**

6 tablespoons (¾ stick) **unsalted butter**

2 sprigs of fresh **thyme**

6 ounces **egg noodles**

2 tablespoons chopped fresh **flat-leaf parsley leaves**

2 cups **cherry tomatoes**, halved

1 teaspoon **balsamic vinegar**

START THE WATER: Bring a large pot of salted water to a boil.

SEAR THE STEAKS: Heat a large cast-iron skillet over medium-high heat. When hot, pour in the oil. Sprinkle the steaks with salt and pepper and sear 2 steaks until browned on one side, about 4 minutes. Remove the steaks from the skillet. Add the other 2 steaks and sear until browned on one side, about 4 minutes. Flip these steaks and return the first 2 steaks to the skillet, raw-side down. Add 2 tablespoons of the butter and the thyme. Once the butter melts, tilt the skillet slightly to pool the liquid, then constantly spoon the butter over the steaks until the meat is medium-rare, about 4 minutes more. Transfer the steaks to a rimmed plate to rest. Keep the skillet handy.

(continued)

COOK THE NOODLES: Add the noodles to the boiling water and cook according to package directions. Reserve ¼ cup of the cooking water and drain. Return the noodles to the pot and toss with 2 tablespoons of the butter and the parsley.

BLISTER THE TOMATOES: Put the tomatoes in the same skillet and blister over medium heat until blackened in spots and softened, about 4 minutes. When the tomatoes are very soft, remove the thyme sprigs and carefully mash the tomatoes with a slotted spoon or potato masher. Stir in the remaining 2 tablespoons butter and the vinegar until incorporated, thinning out with the reserved cooking water if necessary to make a smooth sauce. Season with ½ teaspoon salt.

SERVE: Slice the steaks thinly against the grain and add any juices that accumulate to the tomato sauce. Divide the noodles among 4 plates, set the sliced steak on top, and finish with the tomato butter sauce.

Instead of egg noodles, use strips of raw **zucchini** (shave them with a vegetable peeler) to get a double dose of veggies in.

ITALIAN GYROS
WITH YOGURT AND TOMATO

Zesty, spicy gyro meat is traditionally made with lamb, seasoned and pressed onto a spit, and carved into crisp-edged slices to serve. Here, sweet Italian sausages, already seasoned with fennel, paprika, and garlic, are split and seared for the same crisp-tender contrast.

- 4 links **sweet Italian sausage** (about 12 ounces)
- 2 teaspoons ground **cumin**
- 1 teaspoon dried **oregano**
- 1 tablespoon **extra-virgin olive oil**
- 2 **tomatoes**, chopped, with juices
- 4 medium **romaine leaves**, chopped (about 2 cups)
- ½ cup plain **Greek yogurt**
- 1 teaspoon fresh **lemon juice**
- ½ teaspoon **harissa**
- ¼ teaspoon **kosher salt**
- 4 (6-inch) round **flatbreads**, such as pocketless pita

SET UP: Preheat a cast-iron grill pan or griddle over medium-high heat.

SEAR THE SAUSAGES: Slice the sausages lengthwise and open them like a book. Remove the casings and press the sausages until flattened to about ¼ inch thick. Combine the cumin and oregano in a small bowl. Sprinkle one side of the sausages with the spice mixture. Pour the oil into the pan. Add the sausages, seasoned-side down, and cook each side until the sausages are browned and cooked through, about 3 minutes per side.

MAKE THE TOPPINGS: Toss the tomatoes and their juice with the lettuce in a medium bowl. Stir the yogurt, lemon juice, harissa, and salt in another bowl until smooth.

SERVE: Warm each flatbread in a dry skillet for about 30 seconds per side. Top evenly with the tomatoes and lettuce. Spoon 1 tablespoon of yogurt sauce over each. Put the sausages on the yogurt and serve the extra sauce on the side.

HARISSA is a fiery North African condiment that's found in a tube or a jar. Either way, it lasts nearly forever in the fridge and can be mixed with mayo or yogurt for an easy dipping sauce for meat, vegetables, or even French fries. It's unique and hard to swap out, but if you can't find it, fake it with a combo of Asian chile-garlic sauce and lemon juice.

PREHEATING THE PAN under the broiler helps both sides of the steak cook simultaneously, cutting the cook time almost in half with no flipping necessary.

BROILED PAPRIKA FLANK STEAK WITH TOASTED SPICED NUTS

Smoky paprika mayonnaise cooks into a creamy crust on top of broiled steak. The spiced nut mixture is inspired by the Middle Eastern condiment dukkah, which is a delicious tangy combo of chopped nuts, herbs, and spices usually used as a dip for bread. Save any leftover dukkah to eat with roasted vegetables, cheese, or yogurt.

1½ teaspoons **coriander seeds**

1½ teaspoons **cumin seeds**

¼ cup chopped unsalted **cashews**

¼ cup chopped raw **pistachios**

½ teaspoon crushed **red pepper flakes**

1 tablespoon **sesame seeds**

1 teaspoon **smoked sweet paprika**

3 tablespoons **mayonnaise**

1½ pounds **flank steak**

Kosher salt and freshly ground **black pepper**

Nonstick cooking spray or **vegetable oil**

1 tablespoon chopped fresh **mint**

SEASON THE NUTS: Toast the coriander and cumin seeds in a small skillet over medium heat until fragrant, about 2 minutes. Pour into a bowl to cool, then pulse in a spice grinder until fine. Toast the cashews and pistachios in the same skillet, stirring occasionally to prevent burning, until browned, about 5 minutes. Transfer the nuts to a bowl and toss with the toasted ground spices and red pepper flakes. Toast the sesame seeds in the same skillet until fragrant and browned, about 3 minutes. Add to the spiced nuts.

SET UP: Preheat the broiler to high with a rack set 6 inches from the heat source.

SEASON THE STEAK: Stir the paprika into the mayonnaise in a small bowl until smooth. Sprinkle the flank steak with salt and pepper, then evenly spread the paprika mayonnaise on top of the meat. Set aside for 15 minutes.

BROIL THE STEAK: Meanwhile, set a broiler pan or a heavy baking sheet under the heating element and preheat for 5 minutes. Carefully spray the hot pan with cooking spray or brush lightly with vegetable oil and quickly put the meat on the pan. Broil until a thermometer inserted sideways into the thickest part of the meat reads 130°F to 135°F and the mayonnaise is deep brown and bubbly, 5 to 7 minutes. Remove from the broiler and let the steak rest for 5 minutes before slicing.

SERVE: Slice the meat thinly against the grain. Stir the mint into the spiced nuts and scatter some on top of the steak. Put the rest of the spiced nuts in a bowl to serve on the side for sprinkling.

SERVES 4

ACTIVE TIME

25 minutes

TOTAL TIME

45 minutes

We're starting to see more **PORK SHOULDER** steaks in stores. They're a quick-cooking, flavorful cut that gets all the good flavor you normally see in long-cooked shoulder stews. If you can't find them, chops (any kind— loin, rib, or T-bone) will work just as well.

CUMIN PORK STEAK
WITH GRILLED SAVOY CABBAGE AND APPLES

Grated onion tenderizes flavorful pork shoulder steaks (or regular pork chops, if you have them) in this smoky, all-grill dinner that screams fall.

½ medium **onion**
1 tablespoon ground **cumin**
1 teaspoon ground **coriander**
1 teaspoon dried **oregano**
4 (¾-inch-thick) **pork shoulder steaks** (about 8 ounces each)
⅓ cup **applesauce**
1 tablespoon **red wine vinegar**
½ cup **extra-virgin olive oil**, plus more for brushing
Kosher salt and freshly ground **black pepper**
2 firm **red apples**, such as Braeburn or Gala, cored
1 small head **savoy cabbage** (about 1 pound)

SET UP: Prepare a grill or grill pan and heat to medium-high heat.

MARINATE THE PORK: Grate the onion on the large holes of a box grater into a large ceramic or glass baking dish. Squeeze the excess liquid from the onion, keeping the onion juice in the baking dish and putting the onion in a medium bowl. Whisk the cumin, coriander, and oregano into the onion juice. Add the steaks, toss to coat, and set aside to marinate for 20 minutes at room temperature.

MAKE THE DRESSING: Whisk together the grated onion, applesauce, vinegar, and oil. Season with salt and pepper.

GRILL THE PORK: Sprinkle the pork with salt and pepper on both sides. Grill the steaks to medium (an instant-read thermometer inserted sideways should register 145°F), 5 to 7 minutes per side. Let rest while you make the salad.

(continued)

PREP THE SALAD: Cut each apple into 8 equal wedges. Cut the cabbage into 8 wedges (leave the core intact so the leaves stay together). Brush the apples and cabbage lightly with some of the dressing and grill, covered, until tender and slightly charred, 3 to 4 minutes per side.

SERVE: Divide the cabbage wedges among 4 plates and drizzle with some of the dressing.

Change just a few seasonings for a whole new spin on these steaks. To make it Oktoberfest-style, add 1 tablespoon of grainy mustard to the marinade, skip the cumin, then add caraway in place of the oregano. For smoke lovers, cut the cumin in half and replace with smoked paprika, then add 1 to 2 teaspoons pureed chipotle in adobo to the dressing (for even more smoke, replace the oil with an equal amount of warm bacon fat).

TEN FUN
PAN SAUCES

PAN SAUCES work wonders for just about any piece of meat, fish, or poultry sautéed on the stovetop. Once you know the basics, it's easy to riff. And riff you should. See the following chart for suggested proportions, or play by ear.

After cooking your meat, poultry, or fish, take it out of the pan. The little **brown bits** left in the pan will be the base of your sauce. Pour out all but a couple tablespoons of the fat that's left in your pan (or add some if needed).

Add chopped-up **aromatic vegetables** (like onion, garlic, shallot, ginger, or scallion) to the fat and cook over medium heat until softened.

Add a **deglazing liquid** (usually acidic) like lemon juice, vinegar, or wine, and use a wooden spoon to scrape up the brown bits. Simmer until the liquid has thickened and evaporated by half.

Add the **main liquid,** like stock, broth, juice, or cream, and simmer to reduce until the sauce is thick enough to coat your protein.

Swirl in a bit of **richness** (like cold butter, extra-virgin olive oil, cream, or cheese) to round out the flavor.

Add a **finishing flavor** (like mustard, herbs, or citrus).

(continued)

(continued from page 99)

TEN FUN PAN SAUCES

PAN SAUCE Serves 4	=	AROMATICS (cook in pan drippings)	+	DEGLAZING LIQUID (stir, scrape and reduce)
MUSTARD PICKLE (for chicken, beef, or pork)		¼ cup chopped **onions**		¼ cup **pickle juice**
SWEET VINEGAR GARLIC (for any meat or fish)		2 tablespoons each chopped **garlic** and **ginger**		2 tablespoons each **rice vinegar** and **soy sauce**
MEXICAN BEER (for steak or pork)		2 tablespoons each minced **garlic** and diced **jalapeño**		¼ cup pale **Mexican beer**
ALMOND WINE (for chicken or pork)		2 tablespoons each chopped **garlic** and **scallions**		¼ cup **white wine**
POMEGRANATE (for fish, chicken, or pork)		¼ cup chopped **shallots**		¼ cup **balsamic vinegar**
MUSHROOM GOAT CHEESE (for chicken or pork)		3 tablespoons mixed sliced **mushrooms** 1 tablespoon minced **shallots**		¼ cup **red wine**
OLD-FASHIONED (for steak or pork)		3 tablespoons minced **shallots** 1 tablespoon minced fresh **rosemary**		¼ cup **bourbon**
CREAMY APPLE DIJON (for chicken or pork)		2 tablespoons each chopped **onion** and diced **apples**		¼ cup **Calvados** or **brandy**
LEMON DILL (for chicken or fish)		2 tablespoons each minced **shallots** and **garlic**		¼ cup **white wine**
COGNAC HORSERADISH CREAM (for steak, pork, or chicken)		¼ cup minced **garlic**		¼ cup **Cognac**

Choosing a flavor may be the hardest part; the rest is simple.

MAIN LIQUID (add and reduce more)	RICHNESS (swirl in)	FINISHING FLAVOR (customize)
½ cup **chicken broth**	2 tablespoons **unsalted butter**	2 teaspoons each chopped fresh **dill** and **dill pickles** 2 tablespoons **whole-grain mustard**
½ cup **mirin** (Japanese rice wine) or **sake**	2 teaspoons **toasted sesame oil**	1 to 2 **scallions**, sliced
½ cup **beef broth** dash of **Worcestershire**	2 tablespoons **cream**	2 teaspoons chopped fresh **cilantro** squeeze of **lime**
¼ cup each **chicken broth** and **cream**	¼ cup grated **Parmesan**	2 tablespoons sliced **almonds** 1 teaspoon each fresh **lemon juice** and chopped **tarragon**
½ cup **pomegranate juice**	2 tablespoons **unsalted butter**	2 teaspoons chopped fresh **rosemary** 2 tablespoons **pomegranate seeds**
½ cup **beef broth**	¼ cup **fresh goat** or other **creamy cheese**	2 tablespoons chopped fresh **thyme**
½ cup **orange juice**	2 tablespoons **unsalted butter**	¼ cup chopped **cherries** grated zest of ½ **orange**
½ cup **apple cider**	2 tablespoons **crème fraîche**	2 teaspoons each chopped fresh **thyme** and **rosemary** 2 tablespoons **Dijon mustard**
½ cup **chicken broth**	2 tablespoons **unsalted butter**	1 tablespoon each grated **lemon zest** and **juice** 2 tablespoons chopped fresh **dill**
½ cup **chicken broth**	¼ cup **heavy cream**	1 tablespoon **prepared horseradish**

PRETZEL-MUSTARD-CRUSTED PORK TENDERLOIN SLIDERS

Mustard and pretzels make a crispy, salty breading for pounded pork tenderloin. These are a great game-day snack paired with a cold beer.

3 cups **pretzel crackers**, finely crushed (1¼ cups crushed pretzels)

½ cup **whole-wheat** or **all-purpose flour**

Flaky sea salt, such as Maldon

2 large **eggs**

1 tablespoon **Dijon mustard**

⅓ cup **mayonnaise**

3 tablespoons chopped **bread-and-butter pickles**, plus 24 whole slices

1 tablespoon prepared **horseradish**

2 teaspoons **hot sauce**

1 small **pork tenderloin** (about 1 pound)

Vegetable oil, for frying

12 **slider rolls**

Iceberg lettuce leaves, for garnish

PREPARE THE BREADING: Stir the pretzel crumbs, flour, and 1 teaspoon salt together in a 9 by 13-inch baking dish. Whisk the eggs and mustard in a medium bowl.

MAKE A SAUCE: Combine the mayonnaise, chopped pickles, horseradish, and hot sauce in a small bowl.

BREAD THE PORK: Cut the pork tenderloin crosswise into 12 even pieces about ¾ inch thick. Lay the pieces between sheets of plastic wrap and pound with a mallet until flattened into rounds roughly 2½ inches in diameter and ¼ inch thick. Press both sides of the pork into the pretzel flour, then dip each piece into the beaten eggs and again in the pretzel flour, until generously coated.

FRY THE PORK: Heat ¼ inch of oil in a large skillet over medium-high heat until shimmering (about 375°F). Line a plate with paper towels. Shallow-fry half of the pork cutlets until golden brown on each side,

about 2 minutes per side. Transfer to the prepared plate to drain. Season generously with salt. Repeat with the remaining cutlets.

SERVE: Toast the rolls if desired and put a pork cutlet on each roll. Top each piece of pork with 1 rounded teaspoon sauce, 2 pickle slices, and a piece of lettuce.

Q:

WHAT IS
YOUR MOST
INDISPENSABLE
KITCHEN TOOL?

A:

"My Microplane. I
use it for everything
from spices to
ginger, garlic, lemon
zest; it's a small tool
that has the power
to unleash big
flavors."

—JUDGE MANEET
CHAUHAN

GARLIC AND VINEGAR GLAZED PORK CHOPS WITH SCALLIONS

Sweet-and-sour pork marinade does double duty in this recipe; after flavoring the meat, it gets cooked down into a quick and easy glaze for the pork and peppers.

½ cup **soy sauce**

½ cup **cider vinegar**

2 tablespoons **brown sugar** or **molasses**

3 **garlic cloves**, finely grated

2 **scallions**, chopped (white and green parts)

4 (¾-inch-thick) **pork rib chops**, bone-in
   (about 1½ pounds total)

2 tablespoons **extra-virgin olive oil**

2 red, yellow, or orange **bell peppers**, or a mix, sliced

Kosher salt and freshly ground **black pepper**

2 cups cooked **white rice**, for serving

SET UP: Preheat the broiler to high with the rack about 4 inches from the heat source.

MARINATE THE PORK: Combine the soy sauce, vinegar, brown sugar, garlic, and scallions in a resealable plastic bag. Add the pork chops and massage the marinade into the meat. Marinate for 20 minutes at room temperature or for up to 2 hours in the refrigerator.

SAUTÉ THE PEPPERS: Meanwhile, heat a medium skillet over medium heat. Add the oil, bell peppers, ½ teaspoon salt, and a couple turns of pepper. Cook until softened, about 4 minutes. Transfer to a medium bowl.

REDUCE THE SAUCE: Pour the marinade from the bag into a medium saucepan, bring to a boil, and boil for 1 minute. Pour half of the mixture over the peppers. Continue reducing the remaining sauce until thickened to a glaze, about 5 minutes more.

BROIL THE PORK: Put a foil-lined broiler pan or baking sheet under the broiler to heat for 5 minutes. Put the chops on the pan and brush with the glaze. Broil the chops, brushing with more glaze every 2 minutes, until the chops are cooked through and slightly charred, about 8 minutes. Bring any remaining glaze to a boil and cook for 1 minute.

SERVE: Put each chop over ½ cup of rice per plate. Top with the sautéed peppers and drizzle with extra glaze.

To turn this dish into a speedy **STIR-FRY,** cut boneless **pork chops** into ¼-inch-thick slices. Mix the **soy, vinegar, sugar, garlic,** and **scallilons** together with 1 tablespoon of **cornstarch** and set aside to make a sauce. The rest is easy: Heat some **vegetable oil** until really hot and quickly stir-fry 3 **peppers** until crisp-tender, about 3 minutes, then add the pork and stir-fry for 1 minute. Add the sauce, let it boil for a minute or two, and serve over **rice.**

BEAT-THE CLOCK STIR-FRY

QUICK SKILLET KIELBASA
PORK AND BEANS

Hot dog buns double as croutons in this smoky-sweet take on pork and beans. Already-cooked kielbasa just needs to be browned and heated before serving.

1 tablespoon **vegetable oil**

1 pound **kielbasa**, cut into ½-inch rounds

1 medium **onion**, diced (about 1 cup)

3 ounces **tomato paste** (⅓ cup)

2 tablespoons **dark brown sugar**

2 tablespoons **balsamic vinegar**

1 tablespoon chopped **chipotle in adobo**

2 (14-ounce) cans **navy beans**, with liquid

Kosher salt and freshly ground **black pepper**

2 **hot dog buns**, cut into ½-inch cubes

2 tablespoons **unsalted butter**, melted

¼ cup **pickle relish**

SEAR THE SAUSAGE: Heat a large skillet over medium-high heat. When hot, pour in the oil. Add half of the kielbasa rounds, cut-side down, and cook until browned, about 2 minutes. Flip and cook for 1 minute more. Transfer to a paper-towel-lined plate. Cook the remaining rounds until both sides are browned. Add to the plate. Reduce the heat to medium, add the onion, and cook until softened and slightly browned, about 5 minutes.

SET UP: Preheat the broiler to high with a rack set 4 inches from the heat source.

SIMMER THE BEANS: Whisk the tomato paste, brown sugar, vinegar, and chipotle into the onion. Pour half a can of beans (including the bean liquid) into the skillet and mash with a fork until creamy. Then add the rest of the beans, the kielbasa, ½ cup water, 1 teaspoon salt, and a couple turns of pepper. Simmer until thick and creamy, about 20 minutes.

TOAST THE BREAD: Toss the hot dog bun cubes with the melted butter on a baking sheet and season with salt and pepper. Broil until toasted and browned, flipping occasionally, about 2 minutes.

SERVE: Divide the kielbasa and beans among 4 bowls. Top evenly with the hot dog bun croutons and pickle relish.

RAMP UP YOUR
POT ROAST

Pot roast, which cooks long and slow, is the opposite of a flash in the pan, but provides so much satisfaction with so little effort. If you have a few hours and a hearty cut of meat (pork shoulder, beef brisket, chuck, or even short ribs), try one of these three ways to turn classic pot roast into a whole new dish. What makes a braise like this so good for Sunday cooking and entertaining is that most of the work happens long before people sit down to eat, freeing you to freak out about more pressing things, like where you put the extra wineglasses. Serve with Mustard Smashed Potatoes (page 88).

1 **PREHEAT** the oven to 350°F. Heat a Dutch oven or a large, heavy-bottomed pot over medium-high heat. When hot, pour in 3 tablespoons **vegetable oil**. Sprinkle a 4-pound boneless **chuck roast** generously with **kosher salt** and freshly ground **pepper**. Sear the beef until browned on all sides, about 8 minutes. Transfer to a plate.

2 **THEN** choose one of these combinations:

ITALIAN FENNEL

Add 1 sliced large bulb **fennel** (reserve the fronds), 3 **celery stalks** cut into 1-inch pieces, 1 chopped large **onion,** 5 sliced **garlic cloves,** and 2 **bay leaves** to the drippings in the Dutch oven and cook until slightly browned, about 10 minutes. Pour in 1 cup **red wine** and stir until reduced by half. Stir in 2 cups **chicken broth,** 1 (28-ounce) can whole peeled **tomatoes** (crushed by hand), and 3 sprigs each fresh **parsley, thyme,** and **basil.** Skip to step 3. **To serve,** slice the pot roast and arrange over **polenta** or pasta, garnished with the **fennel fronds.**

GOULASH

Add 3 **celery stalks** cut into 1-inch pieces, 1 chopped large **onion,** 1 large **parsnip** cut into 1-inch pieces, 5 sliced **garlic cloves,** and 2 **bay leaves** to the drippings in the Dutch oven and cook until slightly browned, about 10 minutes. Add 2 tablespoons **tomato paste** and about 2 teaspoons **sweet paprika;** cook until darkened, 2 minutes. Pour in 1 cup dry **white wine** and stir until reduced by half. Stir in 2 cups **chicken broth,** 2 tablespoons **prepared horseradish,** and 3 sprigs each fresh **parsley** and **thyme.** Skip to step 3. **To serve,** slice the pot roast, add ⅓ cup **yogurt** and 2 more tablespoons **prepared horseradish** to the sauce, and arrange over **egg noodles** or mashed potatoes.

BEER AND ONION

Cook 3 chopped slices of **bacon** until crispy; reserve for garnish. Add 3 chopped medium **onions,** 5 sliced **garlic cloves,** and 2 **bay leaves** to the drippings in the Dutch oven and cook until slightly browned, about 10 minutes. Stir in 2 tablespoons **all-purpose flour** and cook for 2 minutes. Slowly pour in 1 (12-ounce) bottle **amber ale** and stir until thickened. Stir in 2 cups **beef broth.** Skip to step 3. **To serve,** slice the pot roast and serve with **crusty bread** or Gruyère/Swiss cheese toasts.

3 **RETURN** the browned beef to the Dutch oven. Bring to a simmer, cover, transfer to the oven, and braise, flipping halfway through the cooking time, until the meat is fork tender, about 3½ hours. Skim off and discard the fat from the top of the sauce before serving. Discard any whole herbs.

COMPLETELY FUN WAYS
TO COOK
VEGETABLES

Trying to eat more vegetables? This is your chapter. Almost all of these speedy dishes are equally comfortable as stand-alone meals that happen to star vegetables, as they are as sides. (The ones that aren't just need a bit of protein to turn them into dinner.)

BEETS

BEET and RED CABBAGE SLAW • ROASTED BEET and ORANGE SALAD with
BEET GREENS and WALNUTS • SALT-ROASTED BEETS with HORSERADISH
SOUR CREAM

BELL PEPPERS

GREEK BELL PEPPER SALAD • PEPPER CAPONATA •
PEPPER and QUINOA SALAD

BRUSSELS SPROUTS

SHAVED RAW BRUSSELS SPROUTS with RED PEPPERS, PEANUTS, and
SWEET CHILE DRESSING • CREAMED BRUSSELS SPROUTS • ROASTED
BRUSSELS SPROUTS with SALAMI, POTATOES, and ONIONS

BROCCOLI

TOASTED COUSCOUS BROCCOLI SLAW with BUTTERMILK DRESSING •
BRAISED BROCCOLI with CHICKPEAS and OLIVES •
SOUTHEAST ASIAN CHARRED BROCCOLI

CARROTS

MAPLE-GLAZED CARROTS • MOROCCAN CARROT SALAD •
LEMON ROASTED CARROTS

CAULIFLOWER

TOASTED CAULIFLOWER with SERRANO HAM and ALMONDS •
CAULIFLOWER and CANNELLINI BEAN MASH • GRILLED CAULIFLOWER
STEAK with TOMATO RELISH

CELERY

CELERY and MELON SALAD with LEMON DRESSING •
BRAISED CELERY and LEEKS with VANILLA • BROILED CELERY and
CHERRY TOMATOES with SHAVED PARMESAN

CORN

ROASTED CORN and CHICKPEA SALAD • CORN ON THE COB with
SWEET and SPICY YOGURT SAUCE • COCONUT CREAMED CORN

CREMINI MUSHROOMS

CREMINI CARPACCIO • STIR-FRIED MUSHROOMS with
KETCHUP-GINGER SAUCE • QUICK PICKLED BABY CREMINI

GREEN BEANS

GREEN BEAN and COCONUT STIR-FRY • GREEN BEAN TEMPURA with
AVOCADO MAYO • SOUTHERN STEWED GREEN BEANS and KALE

POTATOES

SKILLET POTATO PANCAKES • BUTTERY ROASTED POTATOES
with WILTED SPINACH • EASY CAESAR POTATO SALAD

ROMAINE LETTUCE

LETTUCE SOUP • GRILLED WEDGE with BACON and BLUE CHEESE •
BUFFALO SAUTÉED ROMAINE

TOMATOES

PICO DE GALLO STACKS • TOMATO-CHEDDAR GRATIN • BLISTERED
CHERRY TOMATOES with PARMESAN SOUR CREAM and TOASTED BREAD

BUTTERNUT SQUASH

SHAVED BUTTERNUT SQUASH SALAD • BUTTERNUT COCONUT CURRY •
SAUSAGE-STUFFED BUTTERNUT ROAST

ZUCCHINI

LEMONY SPAGHETTI and ZUCCHINI • ZUCCHINI TART •
GRILLED BREADED ZUCCHINI WEDGES

GETTING GOOD VEGETABLES

Everything's easier with good-quality veggies—all you have to do is showcase their natural flavors. Here's how to pick the best, and what to do with them once you get home.

BEETS

Look for: firm, uniform shape and size (not too big) with bushy, lush tops
Store: greens and roots separately; eat greens within a day or two and keep roots in a perforated plastic bag in the crisper drawer, for up to 2 weeks
Bonus: potassium

BELL PEPPERS

Look for: brightly colored heavy ones with smooth stems, taut skin, and no browning around the stem
Store: in the fridge for up to four days
Bonus: vitamin C

BROCCOLI

Look for: vibrant color and tightly closed florets; no yellowing, bruising, or wilting
Store: unwashed in a plastic bag in the crisper for up to a week
Bonus: vitamin A, vitamin C, vitamin K

BRUSSELS SPROUTS

Look for: tight heads, vibrant green color, no brown leaves or holes
Store: in a plastic bag in the fridge for up to a week
Bonus: vitamin A, vitamin C, vitamin K, lutein

BUTTERNUT SQUASH

Look for: firm, hard squash with no soft spots or bruising along the stem
Store: in a dark cool spot for up to several weeks
Bonus: vitamin A, vitamin C, beta carotene

CARROTS

Look for: lush green tops, firm roots, uniform shapes
Store: in a perforated bag in the crisper, with tops removed (greens cause them to soften faster), for up to 2 weeks
Bonus: vitamin A, beta carotene

CAULIFLOWER

Look for: firm, white, tightly closed florets, crisp leaves attached to base, no brown spots or bruising
Store: in a plastic bag in the crisper for up to a week
Bonus: vitamin C, vitamin K, fiber

CELERY

Look for: tight stalks with bushy leaves, ideally organic, no wilting or browning
Store: in the crisper for up to a week; remove any rubber bands
Bonus: vitamin K, lutein

CORN

Look for: heavy ears in the husk, with healthy-looking silks and moist stalk ends; ideally from a farm stand or market
Store: in the fridge with a damp towel on top, but eat ASAP; shuck right before cooking
Bonus: vitamin C, lutein

CREMINI MUSHROOMS

Look for: firm, dry, smooth caps, without black spots, wrinkles, or wetness
Store: in a paper bag in the fridge for up to a week
Bonus: vitamin D, potassium

GREEN BEANS

Look for: firm beans, uniform in color, no seed bumps or bruising
Store: in a sealed container in the crisper, but eat ASAP
Bonus: vitamin A, vitamin C, vitamin K, fiber

POTATOES

Look for: firm and smooth ones with no eyes, wrinkled skin, or discoloration
Store: unwashed, in a cool, dark spot, away from onions, for up to two weeks
Bonus: vitamin C, potassium

ROMAINE LETTUCE

Look for: tight heads, no brown or bruised leaves
Store: in a plastic bag in the crisper for up to a week
Bonus: vitamin A

TOMATOES

Look for: smooth skin, bright color, no wrinkles or bruising; ideally from a farm stand or market
Store: at room temperature (never in the fridge)
Bonus: vitamin A, vitamin C, vitamin K

ZUCCHINI

Look for: firm, smooth skin, without bruises or soft spots
Store: in the fridge for up to a week
Bonus: vitamin C, lutein

BEETS

Salt-roasted beets are a showcase piece perfect for a dinner party, while roasted beet salad and shredded beet slaw bring out beets' tangy, earthy flavors.

BEET AND RED CABBAGE SLAW

Peel 2 medium **beets** and grate on a box grater into a bowl. Add ¼ head shredded **red cabbage.** Heat 2 tablespoons **vegetable oil** in a skillet until hot. Add 1½ teaspoons **caraway seeds** and toast until fragrant, about 1 minute. Toss the vegetables with the caraway oil and 2 tablespoons **cider vinegar.** Season with **kosher salt** and freshly ground **black pepper.** Sprinkle with 2 tablespoons fresh **flat-leaf parsley leaves.**

ROASTED BEET AND ORANGE SALAD
WITH BEET GREENS AND WALNUTS

Reserve the **greens** from 4 medium **beets.** Wrap the beets in foil and roast at 425°F until tender, 1 to 1½ hours. Let cool, then peel and cut into wedges. Very thinly slice the beet greens. Remove the peel and pith from 4 juice **oranges,** then cut the segments from the orange. Toss the segments and any juices with 1 thinly sliced small **shallot,** 1 tablespoon fresh **lemon juice,** the beets and beet greens, and 2 tablespoons **extra-virgin olive oil.** Season with **kosher salt** and freshly ground **black pepper.** Top with ½ cup chopped toasted **walnuts.**

SALT-ROASTED BEETS
WITH HORSERADISH SOUR CREAM

Stir together 8 cups **kosher salt** with 8 beaten large **egg whites** until the salt resembles wet sand. Scoop some of the salt onto a baking sheet and put 4 medium **beets,** tops trimmed, on top. Pack the remaining salt around the beets. Bake at 425°F until the salt has formed a hard crust and is golden brown, 1 to 1½ hours. Let the beets cool to warm (about 1 hour), then break the salt away and peel the beets. Cut into ¾-inch steaks. Stir together ⅓ cup **sour cream** with 1 tablespoon each **prepared horseradish** and fresh **lemon juice.** Season with **kosher salt** and freshly ground **black pepper.** Drizzle the sauce over the beets and top with ½ cup chopped **watercress.**

To keep your cutting board and hands pristine while **WORKING WITH BEETS,** wear gloves and put a sheet of parchment on your cutting board while you work.

BELL PEPPERS

There are several ways to roast a pepper—over a hot grill or gas burner, or under the broiler—but jarred ones work well in a pinch. Any of these dishes can also be served at room temperature.

GREEK BELL PEPPER SALAD

Char 4 **red bell peppers** until blackened. Put in a bowl, cover, and let steam until cool, at least 15 minutes. Discard the skins and seeds and cut into 1-inch strips. Toss with ⅓ cup each crumbled **feta** and chopped **kalamata olives,** 2 tablespoons **extra-virgin olive oil,** 1 tablespoon **olive brine,** and 1½ teaspoons dried **oregano.** Scatter with fresh **basil leaves.**

PEPPER CAPONATA

Char 4 **red bell peppers** until blackened. Put in a bowl, cover, and let steam until cool, at least 15 minutes. Discard the skins and seeds and cut into chunks. Heat ½ cup **extra-virgin olive oil** in a large skillet over medium heat. Sauté 1 chopped small **onion** until softened, about 8 minutes. Remove from the heat, add the roasted peppers, ¼ cup **raisins,** and 2 tablespoons each drained brined **capers** and **balsamic vinegar,** and toss to combine. Season with **kosher salt** and freshly ground **black pepper.** Toss with 2 cups **arugula.**

PEPPER AND QUINOA SALAD

Cook 1 cup **quinoa** in boiling salted water until the grains are tender and begin to open, about 20 minutes. Drain. Seed and stem 2 **red bell peppers** and thinly slice. Mash 1 **garlic clove** to a paste with a pinch of **kosher salt.** Toss the quinoa with the peppers, garlic, ½ cup each toasted **pecans** and fresh **flat-leaf parsley leaves,** 2 tablespoons **extra-virgin olive oil,** 1 tablespoon **cider vinegar,** 1 teaspoon **kosher salt,** a couple turns of freshly ground **black pepper,** and ¼ teaspoon ground **cinnamon.**

BRUSSELS SPROUTS

Turn the pungent sprout into dishes that highlight the mellow, sweet, and meaty side of these mini cabbages.

SHAVED RAW BRUSSELS SPROUTS WITH RED PEPPERS, PEANUTS, AND SWEET CHILE DRESSING

Combine ½ cup each **rice vinegar** and water, 3 tablespoons **honey,** 2 tablespoons **Asian fish sauce,** and ¾ tablespoon crushed **red pepper flakes** in a small saucepan over medium-low heat. Simmer until reduced by half and thickened, about 5 minutes. Thinly slice 1 small **red bell pepper** and then cut into 1-inch pieces. Shred 1 pound **Brussels sprouts** in a food processor. Toss the vegetables with ½ cup each chopped **scallions** (white and green parts), **salted peanuts,** and the dressing until coated.

CREAMED BRUSSELS SPROUTS

Coarsely chop 1 pound **Brussels sprouts.** Heat 2 tablespoons **unsalted butter** in a saucepan over medium heat. Cook 1 chopped **shallot** until soft, about 5 minutes. Add the Brussels sprouts and stir until well coated. Pour in 1 cup **heavy cream,** ½ cup water, 1 **bay leaf,** ¾ teaspoon **kosher salt,** and a pinch of freshly grated **nutmeg.** Simmer, covered, for 15 minutes. Remove the lid and continue cooking until creamy and tender, about 10 minutes. Discard the bay leaf.

ROASTED BRUSSELS SPROUTS WITH SALAMI, POTATOES, AND ONIONS

Cook ¼ cup sliced **salami** in ¼ cup **extra-virgin olive oil** in a small skillet until crispy, about 4 minutes. Reserve the salami. Toss the salami oil with 1½ pounds halved **Brussels sprouts,** 12 ounces quartered small **red potatoes,** and 1 diced **onion** on a rimmed baking sheet. Season with 1¼ teaspoons **kosher salt.** Roast at 400°F, stirring the vegetables halfway through the cooking time, until browned, about 30 minutes. Stir in the reserved salami and a handful of chopped fresh **flat-leaf parsley leaves.**

EACH RECIPE
SERVES 4 TO 6

AND USES

1 bunch of
broccoli
(about
1½ pounds),
outer part of
thick stems
peeled

BROCCOLI

Chopped, braised, and charred: challenge your vision of broccoli with new flavors and textures.

TOASTED COUSCOUS BROCCOLI SLAW WITH BUTTERMILK DRESSING

Put 2 tablespoons fresh **lemon juice** in ½ cup **milk;** let curdle for 10 minutes. Cut the **broccoli** into small pieces and, in two batches, finely chop in a food processor. Cook in a large pot of boiling salted water just until no longer raw tasting, 1 to 2 minutes. Drain in a fine mesh sieve; squeeze out excess water. Toss with the homemade buttermilk and 3 tablespoons each **mayonnaise** and chopped fresh **flat-leaf parsley.** Toast ¼ cup (uncooked) **couscous** in a dry skillet until deep golden brown, about 2 minutes. Add to the broccoli and season with **kosher salt.**

BRAISED BROCCOLI WITH CHICKPEAS AND OLIVES

Cut the **broccoli** into long tree-like pieces, about 3 inches across at the top. Put in a large, wide saucepan with ½ cup drained **chickpeas;** 1½ cups water; 3 tablespoons each **extra-virgin olive oil** and chopped pitted **kalamata olives;** 2 tablespoons each chopped **pickled sweet cherry peppers, olive brine,** and plain **dry bread crumbs;** 1 smashed **garlic clove;** and ½ teaspoon **kosher salt.** Bring to a simmer, cover, and cook over medium-low heat until tender, 12 to 15 minutes.

SOUTHEAST ASIAN CHARRED BROCCOLI

Cut the **broccoli florets** into 1-inch pieces and slice the stems ½ inch thick crosswise; toss with 3 tablespoons **vegetable oil** and 1 tablespoon water. Spread on a baking sheet and roast at 450°F, stirring once, until tender and lightly charred, 20 to 25 minutes. Transfer to a bowl and toss with 2 tablespoons chopped **salted roasted cashews** and 1 tablespoon each **Asian fish sauce,** fresh **lime juice,** chopped fresh **cilantro** or **mint,** and chopped **jalapeño.**

CARROTS

Shaving raw carrots makes for a pretty salad with lots of crunch, while roasting and glazing them brings out their natural sweetness.

EACH RECIPE SERVES 4 TO 6

AND USES

1½ pounds carrots

MAPLE-GLAZED CARROTS

Peel the **carrots** and cut into ½-inch pieces. Melt 2 tablespoons **unsalted butter** in a large skillet over medium-high heat. Cook ¼ cup chopped **onion** until softened, about 3 minutes. Add the carrots, 3 tablespoons each **maple syrup** and water, and ¾ teaspoon each **kosher salt** and **chile powder.** Bring to a simmer, then partially cover and cook until crisp-tender, about 6 minutes. Uncover and simmer until the liquid is reduced and glazy, about 4 minutes more. Sprinkle with fresh **thyme leaves** and freshly grated **nutmeg.**

MOROCCAN CARROT SALAD

Peel the **carrots** and shave into ribbons with a vegetable peeler. Toss with 2½ tablespoons each fresh **lemon juice** and **extra-virgin olive oil,** ¾ teaspoon **kosher salt,** ½ teaspoon each ground **cumin** and **coriander,** and a large pinch each **cayenne** and ground **cinnamon.** Top with chopped fresh **flat-leaf parsley leaves.**

LEMON ROASTED CARROTS

Peel the **carrots** and cut them into sticks. Slice a **lemon** into ¼-inch-thick rounds and remove the seeds. Toss the carrots and lemon rounds with 2 tablespoons **extra-virgin olive oil,** 1 teaspoon peeled and grated fresh **ginger,** ¾ teaspoon **kosher salt,** a couple turns of freshly ground **black pepper,** and a sprig of fresh **thyme,** rosemary, or sage. Roast at 425°F in a rimmed sheet pan, stirring once or twice, until tender and browned in spots, about 25 minutes. Top with grated **Parmesan** before serving.

CAULIFLOWER

Smoky grilled cauliflower steaks, toasted cauliflower "couscous," and fragrant mashed cauliflower add new dimensions to an everyday vegetable. Dinner will never be the same.

TOASTED CAULIFLOWER with SERRANO HAM and ALMONDS

Stir 2 tablespoons **extra-virgin olive oil** and 1 teaspoon **smoked sweet paprika** in a small bowl and microwave until fragrant, about 30 seconds. Grate the **cauliflower** on a box grater (or pulse in a food processor, 8 to 10 pulses). Toast the cauliflower in the paprika oil (discard any paprika from the bottom of the bowl) in a large nonstick skillet over medium-high heat until browned, about 15 minutes, stirring occasionally. Fold in ½ cup chopped **serrano ham** or salami, ¼ cup toasted slivered **almonds,** and 1 table-spoon fresh **lemon juice.** Season with **kosher salt** and freshly ground **black pepper.**

CAULIFLOWER and CANNELLINI BEAN MASH

Roughly chop the **cauliflower** and put in a large lidded saucepan along with one 15-ounce can **cannellini beans** with their liquid, ⅓ cup **milk,** 4 tablespoons (½ stick) **unsalted butter,** and 1 tablespoon minced fresh **rosemary.** Bring to a simmer, cover, reduce the heat to medium-low, and cook until the cauliflower is fork tender, about 15 minutes. Uncover and continue cooking until the cauliflower is soft, about 10 minutes. Mash with a potato masher, then stir in ¼ cup grated **Parmesan.** Season with 1 teaspoon **kosher salt** and freshly ground **black pepper** to taste. Serve with shaved Parmesan over the top.

GRILLED CAULIFLOWER STEAK with TOMATO RELISH

Slice the **cauliflower** into four ½-inch-thick steaks with the stem intact. Put in a ceramic or glass baking dish. Dissolve 3 tablespoons **kosher salt** in 5 cups water and pour over the cauliflower. Set aside for 45 minutes. Simmer ¼ cup **red wine vinegar** with 2 tablespoons **sugar,** 1½ teaspoons crushed **fennel seeds,** and ¼ teaspoon kosher salt in a small pot over medium heat for 5 minutes. Add 2 diced **plum tomatoes.** Cook for 2 minutes more. Drain the cauliflower and pat dry. Brush with **extra-virgin olive oil** and grill the slices over medium heat, covered, until lightly charred, about 6 minutes per side. Serve the relish over the steaks.

CELERY

Take celery out of the crudité tray and into three stand-alone sides that deliver crunch, zest, and comfort, respectively. Peeling celery removes some of the extra chew.

EACH RECIPE
SERVES 4 TO 6

CELERY AND MELON SALAD WITH LEMON DRESSING

Peel and thinly slice 8 stalks of trimmed **celery** on the diagonal into 1-inch half-moons. Cut ¼ small **cantaloupe** into 3 wedges, remove the rind, and thinly slice (about 1 cup). Whisk 3 tablespoons fresh **lemon juice,** 1 teaspoon **honey,** ¼ teaspoon **kosher salt,** a couple turns of freshly ground **black pepper,** and 3 tablespoons **extra-virgin olive oil** in a bowl. Toss the melon, celery, ½ cup **celery leaves,** and 1 tablespoon grated **lemon zest** with the dressing and serve.

BRAISED CELERY AND LEEKS WITH VANILLA

Peel and cut 10 stalks of trimmed **celery** and 1 **leek** (white and light green parts, washed and halved lengthwise) into 3-inch lengths. Layer in a baking dish with 1 cup **chicken broth,** 4 tablespoons (½ stick) **unsalted butter,** and ¼ teaspoon **vanilla extract.** Season with 1 teaspoon **kosher salt** and a couple turns of freshly ground **black pepper.** Cover with foil and braise in a 350°F oven for 30 minutes. Uncover and cook until tender, about 20 minutes more. Top with ¼ cup **celery leaves.**

BROILED CELERY AND CHERRY TOMATOES WITH SHAVED PARMESAN

Peel and cut 12 stalks of trimmed **celery** into 1-inch pieces. Toss with ¼ cup halved **cherry tomatoes,** 2 tablespoons **extra-virgin olive oil,** and 1 teaspoon chopped fresh **thyme.** Season with 1 teaspoon **kosher salt** and a couple turns of freshly ground **black pepper.** Put in a baking dish and broil until browned on the edges, 15 to 18 minutes. Toss with ¾ cup chopped toasted **walnuts** and 2 teaspoons grated **lemon zest.** Top with ½ cup shaved **Parmesan.**

PARMESAN gives a dish so much more than just cheesiness. Packed into each hard, milky brick are saltiness, sweetness, richness, and tons of that savory flavor called umami, which magnifies all other flavors. Always shave it yourself and save the rinds for adding flavor to stews and sauces.

CORN

All three of these recipes showcase corn's natural sweetness, whether by pairing it with a spicy cream, poaching it in coconut milk, or roasting it until nutty.

ROASTED CORN AND CHICKPEA SALAD

Combine one 15-ounce can drained and rinsed **chickpeas** with 4 ears **corn** cut from the cob (about 3 cups). Toss with 1 tablespoon **extra-virgin olive oil,** 1 teaspoon each ground **coriander** and **kosher salt,** and a couple turns of freshly ground **black pepper.** Roast at 400°F in a sheet pan until lightly browned, about 30 minutes. Whisk 1 teaspoon **Dijon mustard** with 2 tablespoons **cider vinegar.** Slowly drizzle in ¼ cup extra-virgin olive oil. Toss the corn and chickpeas in the dressing with 1 bunch sliced **scallions** (white and green parts) and 1 cup halved **grape tomatoes.**

CORN ON THE COB WITH SWEET AND SPICY YOGURT SAUCE

Mix ¼ cup each **Greek yogurt** and **mayonnaise** with 2 teaspoons chopped **pickled jalapeños,** 1 teaspoon **honey,** and the grated zest and juice of 1 **lime.** Rub 4 ears fresh, shucked **corn** with **vegetable oil,** sprinkle with **kosher salt** and freshly ground **black pepper,** and grill over medium-high heat until grill marks appear on all sides, about 12 minutes. Serve warm, spread with the yogurt sauce and garnished with more lime zest.

COCONUT CREAMED CORN

Heat 2 tablespoons **vegetable oil** in a large skillet over medium heat. Add 1 pound thawed frozen **corn kernels,** 3 sliced **scallions** (white and green parts), ½ teaspoon **kosher salt,** and ¼ teaspoon crushed **red pepper flakes.** Cook until softened, about 5 minutes. Add ½ cup each **coconut milk** and water and simmer until thickened, about 5 minutes. Remove from the heat and stir in 1 tablespoon **cider vinegar** and ½ cup fresh **cilantro leaves.**

Q:

WHAT IS YOUR MOST OFF-THE-BEATEN-PATH PANTRY INGREDIENT?

A:

"Coconut milk."

—JUDGE SCOTT CONANT

CREMINI MUSHROOMS

EACH RECIPE
SERVES 4 TO 6

AND USES

1 pound
cremini
mushrooms

Step aside, steak: Mushrooms take the starring role in a delicate, flavorful carpaccio that's the perfect summer appetizer. Prefer your mushrooms cooked? There's a speedy stir-fry and a quick pickle that's a perfect make-ahead picnic snack.

CREMINI CARPACCIO

Thinly slice the **mushrooms** on a mandoline and scatter on a rimmed platter. Chop 3 slices **bacon** and cook in a skillet over medium heat until the fat renders and the bacon is crisp, about 8 minutes. Add 3 tablespoons each **cider vinegar** and **extra-virgin olive oil** to the skillet and stir. Pour the bacon dressing over the mushrooms and toss. Finish with a handful of baby **arugula** or flat-leaf parsley leaves, ½ cup shaved **Parmesan,** and freshly ground **black pepper.**

STIR-FRIED MUSHROOMS
WITH KETCHUP-GINGER SAUCE

Stem and quarter 4 ounces **shiitake mushrooms** and quarter the **creminis.** Stir together 1 tablespoon each **ketchup, mayonnaise,** and water plus 1 teaspoon each **soy sauce, toasted sesame oil, white vinegar,** and peeled and finely grated **fresh ginger.** Heat 2 tablespoons **vegetable oil** in a large skillet over medium-high heat. Add 2 smashed **garlic cloves.** Cook for 30 seconds. Add both types of mushrooms and 2 tablespoons water. Cook, stirring, until the mushrooms are tender and golden, 7 to 8 minutes. Add the sauce and stir to coat. Top with a handful of chopped fresh **cilantro.**

QUICK PICKLED BABY CREMINI

Choose small **mushrooms** (1-inch diameter or less) or halve larger mushrooms. Heat ⅔ cup each **cider vinegar** and water in a medium saucepan with 1 tablespoon each **kosher salt** and **sugar,** ½ teaspoon **cumin seeds,** and 1 sprig of fresh **thyme.** Bring to a simmer, add the mushrooms, and cook for 4 minutes. Transfer to a heat-safe bowl with ½ cup thinly sliced **red onion.** Let stand for 45 minutes or refrigerate, covered, for up to 5 days.

**EACH RECIPE
SERVES 4 TO 6**

AND USES

1 pound
trimmed
green beans

GREEN BEANS

From a classic South Indian dish to American South–style stewed beans, our green bean recipes ring in vegetarian three clever ways.

GREEN BEAN AND COCONUT STIR-FRY

Stir together ¼ cup each **unsweetened grated coconut** and water, 1½ teaspoons **curry powder,** and ¼ teaspoon **cayenne.** Cut the **green beans** into ½-inch pieces. Heat 2 tablespoons **vegetable oil** in a large skillet over medium-high heat. Fry 1 teaspoon each **cumin seeds** and sliced **garlic** until fragrant, 30 seconds. Add the beans and a splash of water. Cook, stirring, until crisp-tender, about 6 minutes. Season with ½ teaspoon **kosher salt.** Add the coconut mixture and cook, stirring, for 2 minutes more.

GREEN BEAN TEMPURA WITH AVOCADO MAYO

Puree 1 ripe Hass **avocado** with ¼ cup water, 3 tablespoons **mayonnaise,** 2 tablespoons fresh **lemon juice,** and ½ teaspoon **kosher salt.** Whisk together ¾ cup each **cornstarch** and **all-purpose flour** and 1½ cups **seltzer.** Put the **green beans** in the batter. Working in batches, deep-fry in 375°F **vegetable oil** until crispy and golden, about 3 minutes. Transfer to a paper-towel-lined plate and sprinkle with kosher salt. Serve with the avocado mayonnaise for dipping.

SOUTHERN STEWED GREEN BEANS AND KALE

Heat 2 tablespoons **extra-virgin olive oil** in a large pot over medium heat. Add ½ chopped **onion** and ½ teaspoon **smoked sweet paprika** and cook until softened, about 5 minutes. Add the **green beans**, 8 ounces **frozen kale,** 3 cups water, and 1½ teaspoons **kosher salt.** Partially cover and simmer until the beans are very tender, about 35 minutes. Season with kosher salt. Serve topped with 1 cup finely chopped **tomato** tossed with 2 teaspoons **cider vinegar** and **hot sauce** to taste.

POTATOES

Roasted with brown butter and mustard, tossed with a creamy Caesar dressing, or grated and fried, here are three new ways to think about potatoes.

SKILLET POTATO PANCAKES

Grate 2 medium **russet potatoes** and 1 **parsnip** into a medium bowl and cover with boiling water. Let stand for 10 minutes. Drain and squeeze dry. Mix in 1 small grated **onion,** 1 large **egg,** ¼ cup **cornstarch,** and 1 teaspoon **kosher salt.** Heat ¼ cup each **extra-virgin olive** and **vegetable oils** in a skillet over medium to medium-high heat. Add 2 tablespoons of the potato mixture and spread out to about 3 inches for each pancake. Brown both sides until crispy, about 5 minutes per side. Serve with ½ cup **plain yogurt** mixed with ½ grated **crisp apple,** 1 tablespoon chopped fresh **flat-leaf parsley leaves,** and 1 teaspoon **honey.**

BUTTERY ROASTED POTATOES
WITH **WILTED SPINACH**

Whisk together 4 tablespoons (½ stick) melted **unsalted butter,** 2 minced **garlic cloves,** and 1 tablespoon **whole-grain mustard.** Toss with 1 pound quartered small **red potatoes.** Roast at 400°F until the potatoes are lightly browned and tender, 20 to 25 minutes. Top with 5 ounces **baby spinach** and return to the oven for 3 minutes. Toss to coat and season with **kosher salt.** Serve warm.

EASY CAESAR POTATO SALAD

Boil 1½ pounds **russet potatoes** until tender in salted water, then peel and cut into chunks. Sprinkle with 1 tablespoon **white vinegar** while warm and season with ½ teaspoon **kosher salt.** Mix 1 cup **mayonnaise,** 1 tablespoon each **Dijon mustard** and fresh **lemon juice,** 1 teaspoon each kosher salt and **sugar,** 2 chopped **anchovies,** and 2 minced **garlic cloves.** Toss with the potatoes. Toast ¼ cup **panko bread crumbs** in 2 tablespoons **extra-virgin olive oil.** Stir in a handful of chopped fresh **flat-leaf parsley leaves.** Scatter over the potatoes.

ROMAINE LETTUCE

Romaine lettuce goes beyond salad with these three ways to spin it. You'll be surprised how a little heat can wake up its flavor.

LETTUCE SOUP

Cut one 12-ounce head of **romaine** into chunks. Cook 4 tablespoons (½ stick) melted **unsalted butter** and ¼ cup **all-purpose flour** along with 1 chopped **onion**, 1¾ teaspoons **kosher salt**, and a couple turns of freshly ground **black pepper** in a large pot over medium heat until the onion is softened, about 6 minutes. Whisk in 4 cups **milk** and simmer for 10 minutes. Stir in the lettuce and cook, turning with tongs, until bright green, about 1 minute. Blend the soup until smooth, about 1 minute, and thin with milk or water as desired. Garnish with shredded raw romaine.

GRILLED WEDGE with BACON and BLUE CHEESE

Cook 8 slices (6 ounces) chopped **bacon** in a skillet over medium heat until crisp, about 8 minutes. Transfer the bacon to paper towels, reserving the fat. Cut 2 **romaine** hearts in half lengthwise and brush with the bacon fat. Grill or broil until just charred on both sides, 2 minutes. Stir together ⅓ cup each **mayonnaise, sour cream,** and crumbled **blue cheese** with 1 tablespoon fresh **lemon juice** and ¼ teaspoon **kosher salt** and a couple turns of freshly ground **black pepper.** Serve the grilled lettuce with the dressing and bacon.

BUFFALO SAUTÉED ROMAINE

Heat 3 tablespoons **unsalted butter** in a large heavy skillet over medium heat until it begins to brown and is fragrant, about 2 minutes. Stir in 1 head of chopped **romaine** in batches and sauté, turning with tongs and adding more as it cooks down, until wilted, about 3 minutes. Stir in 1 to 3 tablespoons Buffalo-style **hot sauce** and season with ½ teaspoon **kosher salt** and a couple turns of freshly ground **black pepper.** Garnish with 2 tablespoons store-bought **fried onions.**

TOMATOES

Fresh tomatoes taste best in summer, when you barely have to do anything to them beyond adding a sprinkle of salt. If you feel like doing more (or it's the off-season), try one of these three ways to make the most of them.

PICO DE GALLO STACKS

Thickly slice 4 large **tomatoes** and season with **kosher salt** and freshly ground **black pepper**. Make 4 stacks of tomatoes, layering ¼ cup chopped **red onion**, ⅓ cup fresh **cilantro leaves,** and 1 tablespoon thinly sliced **jalapeño** between the slices. Stir together ⅓ cup **mayonnaise**, 1 tablespoon chopped **chipotle in adobo,** and 2 teaspoons fresh **lime juice**. Drizzle the tomato stacks with the dressing and crumble **tortilla chips** over the top.

TOMATO-CHEDDAR GRATIN

Pulse 4 (6-inch) **soft corn tortillas** in a food processor to a fine crumb. Sprinkle half the tortilla crumbs evenly in a 1½-quart baking dish. Halve 5 **plum tomatoes** and arrange cut-side up over the crumbs. Sprinkle with 1 tablespoon minced **garlic**, 1 teaspoon chopped fresh **oregano,** and ½ teaspoon **kosher salt** and a couple turns of **pepper**. Top with ½ cup grated **Cheddar**. Toss the remaining crumbs with 1 tablespoon **extra-virgin olive oil** and sprinkle over the top. Broil 5 to 6 inches from the heat until the crumbs are golden, about 10 minutes.

BLISTERED CHERRY TOMATOES WITH PARMESAN SOUR CREAM AND TOASTED BREAD

Put 4 cups **cherry tomatoes** in a large cold skillet with ¼ cup **extra-virgin olive oil**, 3 smashed **garlic cloves**, 2 sprigs of fresh **thyme**, and ¾ teaspoon **kosher salt** and a couple turns of freshly ground **black pepper**. Cook over medium heat until the tomato skins have just burst, about 20 minutes. Brush 4 thick slices rustic **bread** with oil from the skillet and toast under the broiler, turning until golden on both sides, about 1 minute. Stir together ½ cup **sour cream**, ¼ cup grated **Parmesan,** and 1 tablespoon drained and chopped brined **capers**. Season with kosher salt and freshly ground black pepper. Slather the toasts with the sour cream sauce and top with the tomatoes.

EACH RECIPE
SERVES 4 TO 6

AND USES

1 pound
butternut
squash

BUTTERNUT SQUASH

Raw shredded butternut delivers a veggie-forward punch to keep up with the pungent flavors in a salad, while a creamy curry and a meaty bake show its softer side.

SHAVED BUTTERNUT SQUASH SALAD

Peel and seed the **squash.** Thinly slice into matchsticks on a mandoline or shred in a food processor. Zest and juice 2 **limes** into a bowl. Stir in 1 tablespoon each **Asian fish sauce** and **toasted sesame oil** along with 2 teaspoons **sugar,** ¼ teaspoon crushed **red pepper flakes,** and some freshly ground **black pepper.** Toss the squash with the dressing and let stand for 10 minutes. Sprinkle with sliced **scallions** (white and green parts) and season with **kosher salt.**

BUTTERNUT COCONUT CURRY

Heat 3 tablespoons **extra-virgin olive oil** in a large pot over medium-high heat. Stir in 2 chopped **onions,** 4 smashed **garlic cloves,** and 1 tablespoon each chopped **serrano chile** and peeled fresh **ginger.** Cook, stirring often, until golden, about 8 minutes. Peel and seed the **squash** and cut into 2-inch chunks. Add to the pot with one 14-ounce can **coconut milk,** 2 cups **chicken broth,** 1 teaspoon **kosher salt,** and a couple turns of freshly ground **black pepper.** Cover and simmer until the squash is tender, about 25 minutes. Serve with a sprinkle of fresh **cilantro leaves,** a **lime** wedge, and some cooked **rice.**

SAUSAGE-STUFFED BUTTERNUT ROAST

Seed the **squash** and cut into 2-inch chunks. Toss in a large baking dish with 2 tablespoons **extra-virgin olive oil,** 1 pound bulk **hot Italian sausage,** and ½ teaspoon each **kosher salt** and freshly ground **black pepper.** Drizzle with 3 tablespoons **maple syrup** and ¼ cup water, then sprinkle with ⅓ cup **panko bread crumbs.** Roast in a 425°F oven until tender, about 35 minutes. Heat the broiler and brown the top, about 3 minutes more. Sprinkle with 1 teaspoon fresh **thyme leaves.**

 Pre-prepped **SQUASH** is a real time-saver, but for the raw salad, peeling and seeding your own is the way to go.

ZUCCHINI

Here are a few easy ways to make the most of the summer's zucchini harvest, from lemony pasta to a more-indulgent breaded wedge. Summer squash works just as well if that's what you have.

LEMONY SPAGHETTI AND ZUCCHINI

Boil 1 pound **spaghetti** in salted water. Drain, reserving 1 cup cooking water. Thinly slice 1 large **zucchini** (about 1¼ pounds) on a mandoline into planks, then cut the planks into long, thin "noodles." Melt ½ stick **unsalted butter** in a large skillet over medium-high heat. Add the zucchini noodles, 1 tablespoon grated **lemon zest,** 1 teaspoon crushed **red pepper flakes,** and 1 teaspoon **kosher salt** and cook, tossing gently with tongs, until crisp-tender, about 2 minutes. Add the pasta and reserved cooking water and toss to combine. Stir in 3 tablespoons fresh **lemon juice** and 1 cup grated **Parmesan.** Season with salt. Top with more Parmesan before serving.

ZUCCHINI TART

Put a baking sheet in a 375°F oven. Lay one round of refrigerated **pie dough** on a piece of parchment. Slightly raise the edges and crimp. Stir together ⅓ cup **mayonnaise** and 1 tablespoon **Dijon mustard** and spread over the crust. Thinly slice 2 medium **zucchini** into rounds and put in a medium bowl. Toss with 1 teaspoon chopped fresh **thyme,** sprinkle with **kosher salt** and freshly ground **black pepper,** and drizzle with **extra-virgin olive oil.** Arrange the slices over the mayonnaise mixture. Carefully remove the hot pan from the oven. Slide the parchment paper onto the pan and bake until the crust is golden and the zucchini is tender, 20 to 30 minutes.

GRILLED BREADED ZUCCHINI WEDGES

Cut 2 medium **zucchini** lengthwise into 6 wedges each. Mix ½ cup **Greek yogurt** and ¼ cup **milk.** Dip the wedges in the yogurt mixture, then dredge in 1½ cups **panko bread crumbs** seasoned with 1 teaspoon each chopped fresh **thyme** and **kosher salt** and ¼ teaspoon crushed **red pepper flakes.** Spray with **nonstick cooking spray** and grill over medium-high heat until the zucchini is nicely marked and tender, about 5 minutes per side. Season with kosher salt and freshly ground **black pepper.** Serve with **lemon** wedges.

ALL THINGS GROUND:
BEYOND BEEF

Ground beef (and chicken, turkey, and pork) is a week-night go-to for good reason—it's affordable, and you can turn it into burgers, meatballs, meatloaf, and even salad at the drop of a hat. Here's how to spin this every-day essential into a dozen innovative dinners.

BEEF PICADILLO ENCHILADAS

CAJUN SPICED BURGERS

PORK AND EGG STIR-FRY WITH BROCCOLI

PORK BARBECUE MEATBALL
SANDWICHES

SHEPHERD'S STEW WITH DUMPLINGS

MAKE OVER YOUR MEATLOAF

MEAT AND COLLARDS PIZZA

THAI TURKEY LETTUCE WRAPS

TURKEY HAND PIES WITH BUTTERNUT
SQUASH AND KALE

TURKISH CHICKEN TACOS

BEEF PICADILLO ENCHILADAS

Spicy-sweet picadillo—the Latin combination of beef, raisins, and olives—finds its way into enchiladas in this comforting, hearty bake.

⅓ cup **vegetable oil**

1 medium **onion**, diced

1 **green bell pepper**, diced

1 pound 80% lean **ground beef**

1 teaspoon **Chinese five-spice powder**

Kosher salt and freshly ground **black pepper**

1 (14-ounce) can crushed **tomatoes**

¼ cup **green olives**, sliced

¼ cup **golden raisins**

12 (6-inch) **corn tortillas**

2 cups shredded **Cheddar** (about 8 ounces)

½ cup **sour cream**

¼ cup **milk**

SET UP: Preheat the oven to 350°F.

MAKE THE PICADILLO: Heat a large skillet over medium-high heat. Add 1 tablespoon of the oil, the onion, and bell pepper. Cook until softened, about 5 minutes. Add the ground beef, five-spice, 1 teaspoon salt, and a couple turns of pepper. Cook, breaking up the meat, until it begins to brown, about 5 minutes. Stir in the tomatoes, olives, and raisins. Simmer until thickened, about 2 minutes. Season with salt and pepper.

MAKE THE ENCHILADAS: Heat the remaining oil in a small skillet over medium heat. Heat the tortillas, one at a time, in the hot oil until they bubble and darken slightly, about 10 seconds per side. Drain on paper towels. Spread about ½ cup picadillo on the bottom of a 9 by 13-inch baking dish. Put about ¼ cup picadillo and 1 tablespoon Cheddar on each tortilla. Roll tightly and lay them in the baking dish, seam-side down. Spoon the rest of the picadillo over the enchiladas and sprinkle with the remaining cheese. Bake the enchiladas until the tortillas are slightly crisp and the cheese is melted, about 10 minutes.

SERVE: Mix the sour cream and milk until smooth and drizzle on top of the enchiladas.

Some **CAJUN SEASONING** blends include salt and some don't—check yours and adjust your seasoning accordingly.

Since you can't taste raw beef to check the seasoning, fry up a tiny patty and taste it.

CAJUN SPICED BURGERS

Beef burgers get a big flavor boost here from Cajun seasoning, while the classic trinity of Creole cuisine (onions, bell peppers, and celery) makes an appearance as well. Our burger blend of choice is 80% lean ground beef—it has the perfect ratio of juiciness to flavor.

1½ pounds 80% lean **ground beef**

2 teaspoons **Cajun seasoning**

3 **scallions**, sliced (white and green parts)

½ cup **mayonnaise**

2 teaspoons **Dijon mustard**

1 teaspoon **hot sauce**

¼ cup loosely packed fresh **flat-leaf parsley leaves**, chopped

1 **celery stalk**, finely chopped (about ½ cup)

1 medium **yellow onion**, sliced into ¼-inch rounds

1 medium **green bell pepper**, sliced into ¼-inch rings

1 tablespoon **vegetable oil**

4 **sesame seed hamburger buns**, split

SET UP: Prepare a grill or grill pan and heat to medium-high heat.

FORM THE PATTIES: Gently mix the ground beef, Cajun seasoning, and scallions. Form into four ½-inch-thick patties.

MIX THE REMOULADE: Combine the mayonnaise, mustard, hot sauce, parsley, and celery in a small bowl. Refrigerate until needed.

GRILL EVERYTHING: Grill the patties, flipping once, to desired doneness, about 4 minutes per side for medium. Brush the onion and green pepper with the oil and grill the vegetables until lightly charred and tender, about 5 minutes total.

SERVE: Toast the buns on the grill for a minute or so. Put a patty on the bottom bun and top with remoulade. Add some onion and bell pepper, then add the top bun.

PORK AND EGG STIR-FRY
WITH BROCCOLI

Sweet and salty hoisin sauce unifies the flavors in this stir-fry, coaxing robustness (what the Japanese call "umami") out of workaday ingredients. Here, eggs and veggies round out a relatively small amount of pork, turning a meat portion for one or two people into a filling meal for four.

1 tablespoon **hoisin sauce**

1 tablespoon **rice vinegar**

1 tablespoon **cornstarch**

½ cup **chicken broth**

3 large **eggs**

2 tablespoons **vegetable oil**

3 **anchovy fillets**, minced

1 **garlic clove**, minced

1 (1-inch) piece of fresh **ginger**, peeled and minced

1 bunch of **scallions**, chopped (white and green parts kept separate)

8 ounces **ground pork**

1 small head of **broccoli**, cut into 1-inch florets (about 3 cups)

Kosher salt

Hot cooked **white rice**, for serving

BLEND THE SAUCE: Whisk together the hoisin, vinegar, and corn-starch in a medium bowl until well combined, then whisk in the broth.

FRY THE EGGS: Lightly beat the eggs in another bowl. Heat a wok or large nonstick skillet over medium-high heat and, when hot, swirl in 1 tablespoon of the oil. Add the eggs and let cook undisturbed until almost set, about 2 minutes. Flip the eggs and continue to cook until set, about 1 minute more. Transfer the omelet to a cutting board and chop.

STIR-FRY: Pour the remaining 1 tablespoon oil into the wok. Add the anchovies, garlic, ginger, and scallion whites and cook, stirring, for 30 seconds. Add the pork and continue to cook, stirring and breaking

up any clumps, until brown, about 5 minutes. Add the broccoli, a splash of water, and ½ teaspoon salt and continue to cook, stirring, for about 2 minutes. Give the stir-fry sauce a quick whisk and add it to the wok. Bring to a simmer and cook, stirring, until slightly thickened, about 2 minutes. Stir in the omelet and scallion greens and serve over rice.

PICKLED JALAPEÑO BRINE adds tangy heat to sauces and brightens up sautéed greens and salad dressings.

PORK BARBECUE MEATBALL
SANDWICHES

This spicy-sweet Asian-style barbecue sauce is a total fridge-door miracle—jam, mustard, barbecue sauce, and pickled peppers add up to way more than the sum of their parts. Instead of bread crumbs, the meatballs are bound with the ground-up ends of the trimmed rolls.

4 (7-inch-long) **soft hero rolls**

½ cup **milk**

1¼ pounds **ground pork**

1 tablespoon **Dijon mustard**

¼ cup loosely packed fresh **flat-leaf parsley leaves**, chopped

½ teaspoon **Chinese five-spice powder**

Kosher salt and freshly ground **black pepper**

½ cup **barbecue sauce**

⅓ cup **cherry preserves**

1 to 2 tablespoons chopped **pickled jalapeños**, to taste

1 to 2 tablespoons **pickled jalapeño brine**, to taste

2 cups **baby arugula**

SET UP: Adjust an oven rack in the top position and preheat the oven to 375°F. Line a rimmed baking sheet with foil.

MIX THE MEATBALLS: Trim the ends of the hero rolls by about 1 inch. Pulse the ends in a food processor to get soft bread crumbs. Soak ¾ cup of the bread crumbs in the milk (save any extra crumbs for another use), about 5 minutes. Gently mix the pork with the soggy bread crumbs, 2 teaspoons of the mustard, the parsley, five-spice, 1 teaspoon salt, and a couple turns of pepper. Form into 16 meatballs, each about 1½ inches in diameter.

BAKE THE MEATBALLS: Arrange the meatballs at least 1 inch apart on the prepared baking sheet. Bake until fully cooked, about 20 minutes. Turn the oven to broil and cook until the meatballs are nicely browned, 3 to 5 minutes.

MAKE THE BARBECUE SAUCE: Combine the barbecue sauce, the remaining 1 teaspoon mustard, the cherry preserves, jalapeños, jalapeño brine, and ½ cup water in a large skillet over medium heat. Simmer until slightly thickened, about 10 minutes. Add the cooked meatballs to the sauce and toss to coat.

SERVE: Split the hero rolls. Put some meatballs in each, drizzle with extra sauce, and top with baby arugula.

DISCO BALLS

For a New Jersey twist, lose the bread on these sandwiches and serve the **meatballs** and sauce disco-style (or poutine-style, if you're in Canada), over fries with melted cheese. Make the **sauce** and meatballs, using dry **bread crumbs** in place of fresh. Bake a big bag of **frozen French fries** until very crispy and leave them on the sheet tray. Top with the meatballs, sauce, and a cup or two of diced **mozzarella** and pop in the oven until the cheese starts to melt.

SERVES 4 WITH
LEFTOVERS

ACTIVE TIME

35 minutes

TOTAL TIME

50 minutes

SHEPHERD'S STEW
WITH DUMPLINGS

All the flavors of shepherd's pie in a weeknight-friendly format! Store-bought gnocchi replaces mashed potatoes, and fresh mint adds a bright finish.

4 tablespoons (½ stick) **unsalted butter**

1 pound **ground lamb** or **beef**

Kosher salt and freshly ground **black pepper**

2 medium **carrots**, cut into thin coins

1 medium **onion**, diced

4 sprigs of fresh **thyme**

8 ounces **white mushrooms**, quartered

¼ cup **all-purpose flour**

½ cup **white wine**

4 cups **chicken broth**

1 (17.5-ounce) package store-bought **potato gnocchi**

½ cup loosely packed fresh **mint leaves**, chopped

BROWN THE MEAT: Melt 1 tablespoon of the butter in a Dutch oven over medium-high heat. Add the ground meat, ½ teaspoon salt, and a couple turns of pepper and cook, breaking up the meat a little, until lightly browned, about 5 minutes. Transfer to a plate using a slotted spoon and reserve the pan drippings.

SAUTÉ THE AROMATICS: Add the remaining 3 tablespoons butter, the carrots, onion, and thyme to the pan. Cook until they begin to soften, about 5 minutes. Add the mushrooms and cook until softened, about 3 minutes. Sprinkle the flour over the vegetables and cook, stirring, until the flour is toasted, about 1 minute. Add the wine, stirring, and simmer until almost completely absorbed, about 2 minutes.

SIMMER THE STEW: Return the meat to the pan, add the broth, and bring to a simmer. Cook until the sauce thickens and the meat is tender, about 15 minutes. Stir in the gnocchi and cook until warmed through, about 3 more minutes.

SERVE: Ladle the stew into soup bowls and garnish with the mint.

MAKE OVER YOUR
MEATLOAF

Month after month, meatloaf is one of the recipes viewers
search for the most on FoodNetwork.com; everyone's always
looking for upgrades and spins on the classic. Here are our
most recent faves: choose your favorite combo.

1   **PREHEAT** the oven to 400°F. Line a rimmed baking sheet with foil and spray with **cooking spray.**

2   **COMBINE** 2 slices **bacon,** 1 chopped medium **carrot** and **celery stalk,** and ½ **onion** in a food processor and pulse until finely chopped. Transfer the mixture to a bowl and add 1½ pounds **meatloaf mix** (ground pork, beef, and veal).

3   **THEN** choose one of these combinations:

SERVES 4 WITH
LEFTOVERS

ACTIVE TIME

15 minutes

TOTAL TIME

1 hour
10 minutes

TANGY QUINOA MEATLOAF

Add 1 cup cooked **quinoa,** ½ cup **golden raisins,** 2 lightly beaten large **eggs,** 2 tablespoons chopped **dill pickle,** 2 teaspoons each **Worcestershire** and chopped fresh **thyme,** 1 teaspoon **kosher salt,** and a couple turns of **black pepper** to the meatloaf base. Mix until well combined. Skip to step 4, adding 1 tablespoon **pickle brine** to the ketchup glaze.

OATS AND APPLE MEATLOAF

Add ⅔ cup **rolled oats,** ⅓ cup **applesauce,** 2 lightly beaten large **eggs,** 2 teaspoons **Worcestershire,** 1½ teaspoons **kosher salt,** and 1 teaspoon chopped fresh **thyme** to the meatloaf base. Mix until well combined. Skip to step 4, adding a pinch of ground **cinnamon** and another teaspoon **brown sugar** to the ketchup glaze. Lightly sprinkle with additional oats after brushing with the glaze.

CHEESY SALSA MEATLOAF

Add 2 cups **tortilla chips** pulsed in the food processor (about ¾ cup crumbs), ½ cup jarred **salsa,** 1 cup shredded **Cheddar,** 2 lightly beaten large **eggs,** 2 teaspoons each **Worcestershire** and chopped fresh **thyme,** 1 teaspoon **kosher salt,** and a couple turns of **black pepper** to the meatloaf base. Mix until well combined. Skip to step 4, omitting the sugar in the ketchup glaze and mixing in 1 tablespoon jarred salsa. Sprinkle with additional Cheddar after brushing with the glaze.

4   **TO** make a glaze, stir together ¼ cup **ketchup,** 2 teaspoons **brown sugar,** and 1 teaspoon **Worcestershire sauce,** making any adjustments for your variation.

5   **TRANSFER** the meatloaf base to the prepared baking sheet. Form into a 9 by 5-inch loaf. Bake for 30 minutes.

6   **BRUSH** the glaze on the meatloaf and bake until it is golden brown all over and an instant-read thermometer inserted into the center registers 160°F, 20 to 25 minutes more. Let rest for 15 minutes before slicing and serving.

SERVES 6

ACTIVE TIME

20 minutes

TOTAL TIME

45 minutes

TOMATO PASTE is like tomato essence: Its intensely acidic, sweet, salty tomato flavor adds richness and depth to soups, stews, and sauces; its thick creamy texture also makes it a great thickener. Cook it for a couple minutes after adding to a dish to mellow its raw taste.

MEAT AND COLLARDS PIZZA

Collard greens top off seasoned ground beef on this Middle Eastern–inspired flatbread. Use the back of a baking sheet so you can really spread out your dough.

Cornmeal, for sprinkling
1 pound frozen **pizza dough**, thawed and at room temperature
1 small red **onion**, half thinly sliced and half chopped
Kosher salt and freshly ground **black pepper**
¾ teaspoon crushed **red pepper flakes**
½ cup grated **Parmesan**, plus more for sprinkling
5 tablespoons **extra-virgin olive oil**
3 **garlic cloves**, minced
1½ teaspoons **sweet paprika**
3 tablespoons **tomato paste**
6 ounces 80% lean **ground beef**
6 ounces frozen **collard greens**, thawed and drained
Grated zest of 1 **lemon** (about 1 tablespoon)
2 teaspoons fresh **lemon juice**

SET UP: Put an inverted baking sheet or pizza stone on the top rack of the oven. Preheat the oven to 400°F. Lay a sheet of parchment on another inverted baking sheet and sprinkle with cornmeal.

MAKE THE FLATBREAD: Form the pizza dough into a large rectangle the size of the baking sheet and put on top of the parchment. Cover the dough with the sliced onion and season with 1 teaspoon salt, a couple turns of pepper, and ¼ teaspoon red pepper flakes. Sprinkle with the ½ cup Parmesan and drizzle with 3 tablespoons of the oil. Slide the parchment onto the hot baking sheet. Bake until the dough is fully cooked and the top is golden brown, about 25 minutes.

COOK THE BEEF: Heat 1 tablespoon of the olive oil in a large skillet over medium heat. Add the chopped onion, the garlic, paprika, and the remaining ½ teaspoon red pepper flakes and cook until soft and beginning to caramelize, about 4 minutes. Stir in the tomato paste and

ground beef and sprinkle with salt; cook until the beef is no longer raw, about 4 minutes. Add the collard greens, lemon zest, lemon juice, and ¼ cup water and cook until heated through. Season as needed.

SERVE: Spread the beef and collards evenly over the flatbread. Sprinkle with additional cheese, drizzle with the remaining tablespoon oil, and cut into squares.

SERVES 4

ACTIVE TIME
20 minutes

TOTAL TIME
20 minutes

THAI TURKEY
LETTUCE WRAPS

We love spice blends for weeknight dinners—you get complex flavor without having to measure out tons of different spices. They're even great used in surprising ways—like in this Thai-style turkey salad, which uses seafood seasoning and comes together in less than 30 minutes.

2 tablespoons **vegetable oil**
2 **garlic cloves**, minced
2-inch piece fresh **ginger**, peeled and minced
1 bunch **scallions**, sliced (white and green parts kept separate)
1 teaspoon **seafood seasoning**, such as Old Bay
1½ pounds **ground turkey**
¼ cup **Asian fish sauce**
1½ cups diced fresh **pineapple**
½ cup loosely packed fresh **cilantro leaves**, roughly chopped
Juice of 2 **limes**, plus wedges for serving
Hot cooked **white rice**, for serving
1 head of **Boston lettuce**, leaves separated, for serving

MAKE THE FILLING: Heat the oil in a large skillet over medium-high heat. Add the garlic, ginger, scallion whites, and seafood seasoning. Cook until the vegetables start to brown, about 5 minutes. Add the turkey and cook, breaking up with a wooden spoon, until golden, about 5 minutes. Stir in the fish sauce and scallion greens and cook until the liquid is almost completely absorbed, about 5 minutes. Stir in the pineapple, cilantro, and lime juice. Remove from the heat.

SERVE: Spoon the filling over the hot cooked rice and serve with lime wedges and lettuce leaves to make lettuce wraps.

TURKEY HAND PIES WITH BUTTERNUT SQUASH AND KALE

These calzone-inspired hand pies pack up really nicely for lunches and road trips—they're just as good at room temperature as they are hot.

3 tablespoons **extra-virgin olive oil**

6 ounces frozen chunks **butternut squash**, thawed (about 1½ cups)

2 teaspoons **Chinese five-spice powder**

8 ounces **ground turkey**

Kosher salt and freshly ground **black pepper**

6 ounces frozen **kale**, thawed and drained (about 2 cups)

⅓ cup chopped **walnuts**

1 (14-ounce) package refrigerated **pie dough**

1 large **egg**, whisked together with 1 tablespoon water

½ cup **sour cream**

Juice of 1 **lemon**

¼ cup loosely packed fresh **flat-leaf parsley leaves**, chopped

SET UP: Preheat the oven to 400°F. Line a baking sheet with parchment paper.

COOK THE FILLING: Heat the oil in a large skillet over medium heat. Add the butternut squash and five-spice and cook until the squash is hot, about 2 minutes. Add the turkey, 1 teaspoon salt, and a couple turns of pepper. Cook, stirring, until the turkey begins to brown, about 4 minutes. Stir in the kale and cook until heated through, about 5 minutes. Remove from the heat and stir in the walnuts. Season with salt and pepper and cool.

MAKE THE PIES: Unroll both sheets of the pie dough on a work surface. Cut each piece into 4 wedges. Spoon a rounded ¼ cup of the filling onto half of each piece of dough. Fold over and crimp with a fork to make triangular hand pies. Brush the egg wash onto the pies. Put the pies at least an inch apart on the prepared baking sheet. Bake until the dough is lightly browned, 15 to 20 minutes.

MAKE THE SAUCE AND SERVE: Mix the sour cream, lemon juice, parsley, and ¼ teaspoon salt in a small bowl. Serve with the hand pies.

SERVES 4

ACTIVE TIME

30 minutes

TOTAL TIME

30 minutes

As the **ONION SALAD** sits in the fridge, the flavors slowly mellow, lessening the raw onion's sharp bite.

TURKISH CHICKEN TACOS

We love the breaking down of taco boundaries we've seen lately—Korean tacos are one of our favorite flavor combinations. So why not go for a Turkish taco? Coriander, nutmeg, and a lightly marinated onion salad take these tacos partway around the globe.

1 cup loosely packed fresh **flat-leaf parsley leaves**, roughly chopped

1 medium **red onion**, thinly sliced

⅓ cup fresh **lemon juice** (about 2½ lemons)

1 tablespoon plus ½ teaspoon **chile powder**

Kosher salt and freshly ground **black pepper**

2 tablespoons **vegetable oil**

1 medium **carrot**, grated

1½ teaspoons ground **coriander**

½ teaspoon freshly grated **nutmeg**

1¼ pounds **ground chicken**

1 cup plain **Greek yogurt**

8 (6-inch) **flour tortillas**, warmed

MARINATE THE ONION: Combine the parsley, onion, 3 tablespoons of the lemon juice, the ½ teaspoon chile powder, ½ teaspoon salt, and a couple turns of pepper. Refrigerate until needed, or for up to 1 day.

MAKE THE FILLING: Heat the oil in a large skillet over medium-high heat. Add the carrot, coriander, nutmeg, and the remaining 1 tablespoon chile powder. Cook until the spices are fragrant and the carrot begins to soften, about 1 minute. Add the ground chicken and sprinkle with ¾ teaspoon salt and a couple turns of pepper. Cook, breaking up the chicken, until it begins to brown, about 5 minutes. Add ½ cup water, bring to a simmer, and cook until slightly thickened, about 5 minutes. Remove from the heat.

SERVE: Mix the yogurt with the remaining lemon juice. To assemble the tacos, scoop the filling into the tortillas, then top with some onion salad and a dollop of yogurt.

BIG SALADS

HEARTY AND FRESH

These filling, veggie-forward meals make the most of what's in the crisper, balance texture, crunch, and heft, and make sure every bite is interesting. Here, we play with salad greens (like hearty kale), add-ins (like curried couscous), and dressings (like blended avocado) to spin the big salad into a new dinner favorite.

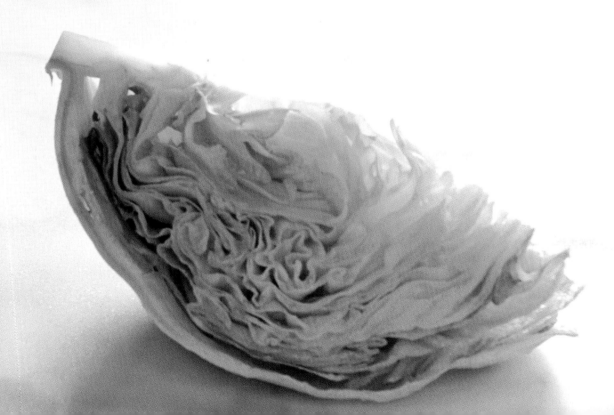

BIBB COBB SALAD

NUTTY TROPICAL KALE AND RICE SALAD

SPICY TACO SALAD

GO-TO GUIDE:
VINAIGRETTES & SALAD DRESSINGS

CHOPPED PANZANELLA

TUNA AND ROASTED POTATO SALAD WITH
AVOCADO BUTTERMILK DRESSING

ROASTED SHRIMP COCKTAIL SALAD

CURRIED ROASTED VEGETABLE AND
COUSCOUS SALAD

If you're cooking both **BACON** and another protein for a recipe, start the bacon in a cold skillet to render as much fat as possible; then reuse the skillet (and the drippings) to cook the other meat.

BIBB COBB SALAD

Tender "butter" lettuces, such as Bibb or Boston, are wonderful in a Cobb salad, while a hard-boiled-egg-based dressing adds richness. Buy a wedge of blue cheese and crumble it yourself; it'll be creamier and more flavorful than purchased crumbles.

3 large **eggs**

5 slices **bacon**

4 (¼-inch-thick) **chicken cutlets** (about 1 pound)

Kosher salt and freshly ground **black pepper**

3 tablespoons **vegetable oil**

3 tablespoons **cider vinegar**

2 teaspoons **Dijon mustard**

2 heads **Bibb lettuce**, leaves separated and large leaves torn

1 **Hass avocado**, sliced

2 cups **grape tomatoes**, halved

4 ounces **blue cheese**, crumbled

BOIL THE EGGS: Put the eggs in a small saucepan and cover with cold water by 1 inch. Bring to a boil over medium-high heat. Boil for 30 seconds, then take off the heat. Cover and let stand for 8 minutes. Drain and rinse under cold water until cool. Crack all over and then peel.

COOK THE MEAT: Put the bacon in a cold skillet and cook over medium heat until crisp, about 12 minutes. Transfer the bacon to a paper-towel-lined plate to drain. Increase the heat to medium-high. Sprinkle the chicken lightly with salt and pepper and add to the bacon drippings in the skillet. Cook, flipping once, until golden brown and cooked through, about 4 minutes per side. Transfer to a plate.

MAKE THE DRESSING: Combine the hard-boiled eggs, ⅓ cup water, the oil, vinegar, mustard, ¾ teaspoon salt, and any accumulated juice from the chicken in a blender and puree until smooth and creamy. Add more water a little at a time to thin if necessary.

SERVE: Crumble or chop the bacon. Cut the chicken into strips. Toss the lettuce with half of the dressing in a large bowl. Top with the chicken, bacon, avocado, tomatoes, and blue cheese. Drizzle with the remaining dressing.

HEARTS OF PALM
are sweet and nutty; we always keep a can in our cupboard for those times when the crisper is bare. They're great with tropical flavors, like the mango in this salad.

NUTTY TROPICAL KALE
AND RICE SALAD

Slicing kale extra-thin helps it get tender enough to eat raw, as does marinating the leaves in a flavorful dressing. Leftover cooked rice adds volume, making this a hearty option for a vegetarian main.

1 large firm ripe **mango**

3 tablespoons **vegetable** or **extra-virgin olive oil**

3 tablespoons **cider vinegar**

Kosher salt and freshly ground **black pepper**

1 pound **kale** (1 to 2 bunches)

1 (14-ounce) can **hearts of palm**, drained and sliced

1½ cups cooked **white rice**, at room temperature

2 medium **tomatoes**, halved and sliced

1 cup mixed **salted roasted nuts**, roughly chopped

MAKE THE DRESSING: Peel the mango and cut the flesh from the pit. Cut half of the mango into ½-inch pieces (about 1 cup) and transfer to a small bowl. Roughly chop the remaining mango and puree in a blender with the oil, vinegar, 2 tablespoons water, ½ teaspoon salt, and a couple turns of pepper.

MARINATE THE KALE: Cut the thick center stem from each kale leaf and discard. Mound a handful of kale at a time on the cutting board and gather it together tightly. Slice crosswise to make very thin ribbons. Put the kale in a large bowl and toss with the mango dressing. Let stand at least 15 minutes and up to 45 minutes to wilt slightly.

TOSS THE SALAD: Add the chopped mango, hearts of palm, rice, and tomatoes, and toss to coat. Season with salt and pepper. Top with the nuts.

SPICY TACO SALAD

SERVES 4

ACTIVE TIME

10 minutes

TOTAL TIME

30 minutes

Bagged slaw—amped up with plenty of cilantro—shreds the prep time on this vegetarian taco salad. The spicy dressing gets its heat and acid from jalapeño brine, and homemade tortilla chips add crunch.

4 (6-inch) **corn tortillas**, preferably white, cut into
   ¼-inch-thick strips
¼ cup **vegetable oil**
2½ teaspoons **taco seasoning**
Kosher salt
2 tablespoons chopped **pickled jalapeños**,
   plus 3 tablespoons brine
1 (14-ounce) bag **coleslaw mix**
2 cups loosely packed roughly chopped fresh **cilantro**
1 cup shredded **Cheddar**
2 medium **tomatoes**, chopped
½ small **red onion**, finely chopped
2 (15-ounce) cans **black** or **pinto beans** (or a mix),
   rinsed and drained
⅓ cup **sour cream**

SET UP: Preheat the oven to 375°F.

CRISP THE TORTILLAS: Toss the tortilla strips on a baking sheet with 1 tablespoon of the oil, 1 teaspoon of the taco seasoning, and ¼ teaspoon salt. Spread in one layer and bake, stirring occasionally, until golden brown and crisp, about 20 minutes.

MAKE THE DRESSING: Heat the remaining 3 tablespoons oil in a small skillet over medium heat. Add the remaining 1½ teaspoons taco seasoning and cook, stirring, until fragrant, about 1 minute. Remove from the heat and stir in the jalapeños, brine, and ½ teaspoon salt.

TOSS THE SALAD: Mix the slaw mix, cilantro, Cheddar, tomatoes, onion, and beans with the dressing. Season with salt. Top with the tortilla strips and dollops of sour cream.

VINAIGRETTES & SALAD DRESSINGS

HOMEMADE DRESSINGS & VINAIGRETTES are one of the easiest ways to add your own flavor twist to a salad. Once you learn how to make one, you can easily make them all. Here are some to start with.

Our go-to ratio for a vinaigrette is **1 part acid to 3 parts oil**. This is not a hard-and-fast rule, since some vinegars are more tart and some oils are more flavorful than others. So, taste often and go with what best suits your taste buds. Mustard blunts the sharpness of vinegar and helps oil and vinegar combine, so if you're including mustard, you might want to adjust the vinegar up or down.

To make a vinaigrette, dissolve a nice pinch of kosher salt in 1 part **acid.** Add a **flavor agent** like mustard and gradually whisk in 3 parts **oil.** Season with freshly ground black pepper. Start with a little less dressing than you think you'll need on your salad—about a scant tablespoon per couple handfuls of greens—then toss to coat, taste, and add more if needed. Leftover dressing keeps in the fridge for a few days.

For creamy dressings, the ratio is more flexible. Just whisk 3 parts **creamy** with 1 part **aromatics,** add **liquid** to thin until it coats a lettuce leaf, and season with kosher salt and a little freshly ground black pepper.

(continued)

(continued from page 165)

VINAIGRETTES (each makes about 1 cup, enough for about 12 salads)

VINAIGRETTE =	ACID (plus a pinch of salt and pepper)	+ FLAVOR AGENT	+ OIL
CLASSIC (good for mixed greens or baby arugula)	¼ cup **white wine vinegar**	1–2 tablespoons **Dijon mustard**	¾ cup **extra-virgin olive oil**
HERB (good for romaine or escarole)	¼ cup **fresh lemon juice** (about 2 lemons)	2 tablespoons chopped fresh **herbs** 1 generous tablespoon **honey**	¾ cup **extra-virgin olive oil**
GOAT CHEESE (good for baby spinach or baby kale)	¼ cup **cider vinegar**	2 tablespoons fresh **goat cheese**	¾ cup **extra-virgin olive oil**
BACON-CITRUS (good for iceberg or spinach)	¼ cup **cider vinegar**	2 teaspoons **sugar** 2 tablespoons fresh **orange juice** generous teaspoon fresh **lime juice**	¾ cup **warm bacon fat**
BASIL-BALSAMIC (good for anything with tomatoes, or for mesclun)	¼ cup **balsamic vinegar**	2 tablespoons chopped fresh **basil** 2 teaspoons minced **garlic**	¾ cup **extra-virgin olive oil**
ITALIAN (good for escarole, red leaf, or green leaf)	¼ cup **red wine vinegar**	2 teaspoons dried **Italian herbs** 2 tablespoons **Dijon mustard**	¾ cup **extra-virgin olive oil**
SPICY ASIAN (good for romaine or butter lettuce)	¼ cup **rice vinegar**	2 teaspoons **Asian fish sauce** 2 teaspoons **Sriracha** 1 teaspoon **sugar** No salt (fish sauce has plenty!)	¾ cup **vegetable oil**
GINGER-SESAME (good for iceberg or romaine)	¼ cup **rice vinegar**	2 teaspoons chopped **pickled ginger** 1 teaspoon **toasted sesame oil**	¾ cup **vegetable oil**
SHERRY-SHALLOT (good for mixed greens or baby kale)	¼ cup **sherry vinegar**	2 tablespoons chopped **shallots**	¾ to 1 cup **extra-virgin olive oil**

SALAD DRESSINGS (each makes about 1 cup)

DRESSING =	CREAMY COMPONENT +	FLAVOR/ AROMATIC +	LIQUID (and salt and pepper)
GARLIC-HERB (good for escarole, romaine, or green leaf)	¾ cup **Greek yogurt**	1 minced **garlic clove** 3 tablespoons chopped **leafy herbs** (parsley, chives, basil, or dill)	2 tablespoons fresh **lemon juice** or water
SPICY DILL (good for baby spinach or baby kale)	¾ cup **Greek yogurt**	1 tablespoon **harissa** 3 tablespoons chopped fresh **dill**	2 tablespoons fresh **lemon juice** ¼ cup **water**
PICKLED (good for watercress or arugula)	¾ cup **Greek yogurt**	2 tablespoons drained brined **capers** 2 tablespoons chopped **pickles**	2 tablespoons fresh **lemon juice** 2 tablespoons **pickle** or **caper juice**
BUTTERMILK-HERB (good for iceberg or romaine)	¾ cup **mayonnaise**	¼ cup chopped **leafy herbs**	¼ cup **buttermilk**
HONEYED DILL (good for watercress and Boston or Bibb)	¾ cup **crème fraîche** or **sour cream**	1 tablespoon **honey** 3 tablespoons chopped fresh **dill**	1 generous tablespoon fresh **lemon juice**
CAESAR (good for romaine)	¾ cup **mayonnaise**	2 tablespoons **anchovy paste** 2 tablespoons minced **garlic** No salt (anchovy paste has plenty!)	2 tablespoons fresh **lemon juice** 2 teaspoons **water**
ASIAN (good for coleslaw mix, iceberg, or romaine)	¾ cup **mayonnaise**	1 generous tablespoon **soy sauce** 1 teaspoon **toasted sesame oil** 1 teaspoon **sugar** 2 tablespoons **black sesame seeds**	2 tablespoons **water**
BLUE CHEESE (good for broccoli slaw, iceberg, or romaine)	¾ cup **mayonnaise**	2 tablespoons **blue cheese** (sometimes if a flavoring is strong, you can use less and add more liquid)	¼ cup **buttermilk**

SERVES 4

ACTIVE TIME

20 minutes

TOTAL TIME

30 minutes

CHOPPED PANZANELLA

This mostly pantry salad is a cross between a classic chopped salad and an Italian bread salad, and the perfect use for stale bread. Grated tomato makes for a bright, fresh-tasting salad dressing base that needs only a splash of vinegar to shine.

4 cups ¾-inch **bread cubes**, preferably stale and from a
    crusty loaf
2 medium to large ripe **tomatoes**
5 tablespoons **extra-virgin olive oil**
1 to 2 tablespoons **red wine vinegar**, to taste
Kosher salt and freshly ground **black pepper**
1 **romaine heart**, chopped into 1-inch pieces
1 cup fresh **flat-leaf parsley leaves**
1 (15-ounce) can **white beans**, rinsed and drained
3 medium **carrots**, chopped
3 **celery stalks**, chopped
2 ounces thickly sliced **salami** or **turkey**, chopped
    (about ⅓ cup)

SET UP: Preheat the oven to 325°F.

DRY THE BREAD: Scatter the bread cubes on a baking sheet. Bake until dried out and hard, but not golden, about 15 minutes.

MAKE THE DRESSING: Halve the tomatoes and grate the cut side on the large holes of a box grater into a large salad bowl, stopping when you get to the skin (discard the skin). Whisk in the oil, vinegar, ¾ teaspoon salt, and a couple turns of pepper.

TOSS THE SALAD: Add the romaine, parsley, white beans, carrots, celery, salami, and bread cubes to the bowl with the dressing and toss to combine. Season with salt and pepper and let sit for 10 minutes before serving.

TUNA AND ROASTED POTATO SALAD WITH AVOCADO BUTTERMILK DRESSING

Lush avocado and tangy buttermilk stand in for dressing in this Southwestern take on a Niçoise salad. This salad works well with any firm lettuce.

12 ounces **baby red potatoes**, halved

1 tablespoon **extra-virgin olive oil**

1 teaspoon **chile powder**

1 firm ripe **Hass avocado**, halved

¾ cup **buttermilk**

1 tablespoon fresh **lemon juice** (about ½ lemon)

½ cup chopped fresh **leafy herbs**, preferably mixed, such as parsley, chives, basil, and dill

Kosher salt and freshly ground **black pepper**

1 head of **romaine**, chopped

1½ cups frozen **corn kernels**, thawed (or kernels from 3 ears fresh corn)

2 **bell peppers**, preferably mixed colors, chopped

2 (5-ounce) cans solid light **tuna** in oil, drained

SET UP: Preheat the oven to 400°F.

ROAST THE POTATOES: Toss the potatoes with the olive oil and chile powder on a rimmed baking sheet and roast until golden brown and tender, about 20 minutes.

MAKE THE DRESSING: Puree half of the avocado in a blender with the buttermilk, lemon juice, herbs, ½ teaspoon salt, and a couple turns of pepper. Chop the remaining avocado half.

TOSS THE SALAD: Combine the romaine with the corn, bell peppers, warm potatoes, and dressing. Season with salt and pepper. Top with the chopped avocado and the tuna, broken into chunks.

"Prepared" **HORSE-RADISH** is the kind you buy in a jar. It's already grated and mixed with vinegar; drain before adding to sauces and dressings. Fresh horseradish is an enormous, knobby root that's intense when freshly grated and mellows over time. Prepared horseradish is more consistently strong-flavored.

ROASTED SHRIMP COCKTAIL
SALAD

Two steakhouse classics—shrimp cocktail and the iceberg wedge—meet in this ultra-fast dinner salad.

1 pound large **shrimp**, peeled and deveined
1 bunch of thin **asparagus**, trimmed
¼ cup plus ⅓ cup **ketchup**
3 tablespoons prepared **horseradish**, drained
1 tablespoon **vegetable oil**
Kosher salt and freshly ground **black pepper**
3 tablespoons **sour cream**
2 **lemons**
¼ cup chopped fresh **flat-leaf parsley leaves**
1 large head **iceberg lettuce**, cut into 4 wedges

SET UP: Preheat the broiler to high with a rack set as close as possible to heat source.

BROIL THE SHRIMP AND ASPARAGUS: Toss the shrimp and asparagus with the ¼ cup ketchup, 2 tablespoons of the horseradish, the oil, and ¼ teaspoon salt and a couple turns of pepper. Spread on a rimmed baking sheet in one layer and broil, stirring once or twice, until the shrimp are just cooked through and both the shrimp and asparagus are lightly charred in spots, about 6 minutes.

MAKE THE DRESSING: Stir together the remaining ⅓ cup ketchup, the remaining tablespoon horseradish, the sour cream, the juice of 1 of the lemons, and 3 tablespoons water. Stir in half of the parsley.

SERVE: Put an iceberg wedge on each of 4 plates and divide the shrimp and asparagus evenly among them. Drizzle with the dressing and sprinkle with the remaining parsley. Cut the remaining lemon into wedges and serve on the side.

CURRIED ROASTED VEGETABLE AND COUSCOUS SALAD

If you have leftover vegetables or couscous, this is the perfect place for them; they add texture and heft to this refreshing salad.

4 medium **carrots**, sliced ½ inch thick on a diagonal
1 small head of **cauliflower**, cut into 1-inch florets
¼ cup **extra-virgin olive oil**
1½ teaspoons **curry powder**
½ teaspoon ground **coriander**
½ teaspoon ground **cumin**
Kosher salt and freshly ground **black pepper**
½ cup **couscous**
½ cup **Greek yogurt**
1 tablespoon fresh **lime juice** (about 1½ limes)
6 cups mixed **baby greens**

SET UP: Preheat the oven to 425°F.

ROAST THE VEGETABLES: Toss the carrots and cauliflower with 3 tablespoons of the oil on a rimmed baking sheet. Combine the curry powder, ¼ teaspoon each of the coriander and cumin, ¾ teaspoon salt, and a couple turns of pepper and sprinkle over the vegetables. Spread in a single layer and roast, stirring once or twice, until crisp-tender and lightly charred, 20 to 25 minutes. Transfer to a bowl and let cool slightly.

COOK THE COUSCOUS: Bring ⅔ cup water to a boil. Add the couscous, the remaining ¼ teaspoon each coriander and cumin, and a pinch of salt. Take off the heat, cover, and let stand for 10 minutes.

MAKE THE DRESSING: Stir together the yogurt, ¼ cup water, the lime juice, the remaining 1 tablespoon oil, and ½ teaspoon salt.

TOSS THE SALAD: Mix the roasted vegetables with the couscous. Drizzle in half the dressing and toss to coat. Toss the greens in the remaining dressing with salt to taste and top with the vegetables and couscous.

FISHING
FOR COMPLIMENTS

We've all seen some pretty out-there fish recipes on *Chopped.* Cream-soda tempura black sea bass? Check. Branzino with fortune cookies? Sure. But we'd rather the fish recipes here become your new quick-cooking, delicious weeknight staples—no bizarre ingredients required.

TILAPIA TARTAR CAKES

MARINATED TILAPIA TACOS

MOROCCAN SPICE BLACKENED CATFISH

MARKET BASKET: FISH

SLOW-COOKED SALMON
WITH OLIVE–BREAD CRUMB SPRINKLE

SUPER-SAUCE GRILLED SALMON
WITH GRILLED SCALLIONS

ALMOND AND WHITE WINE MUSSELS

BROILED TROUT WITH NEW ORLEANS
BROWN BUTTER SAUCE

SHRIMP RAMEN

CONNECTICUT-CAJUN SHRIMP ROLLS

TILAPIA TARTAR CAKES

These fish cakes come with their own condiment built in; all the flavors of tartar sauce are blended into each patty. Try these on a bun for a sandwich, too.

4 slices **white bread** (or 2 hamburger buns)
1 **lemon**
1 pound skinless **tilapia fillets**, cut into chunks
½ cup chopped **sweet pickles**
⅓ cup **mayonnaise**
1 large **egg**, lightly beaten
Kosher salt and freshly ground **black pepper**
5 tablespoons **extra-virgin olive oil**
4 cups **baby greens** or 1 head of **frisée**

MAKE THE BREAD CRUMBS: Pulse the bread in a food processor until finely ground. Scoop 1 cup of the bread crumbs into a medium bowl and spread the remaining bread crumbs (about ¾ cup) on a large plate. Grate the zest of the lemon into the bowl.

FORM THE FISH CAKES: Pulse the fish in the food processor until roughly chopped (do not form a paste), about 14 pulses. Add the fish to the bowl with the bread crumbs along with the pickles, mayonnaise, egg, ¾ teaspoon salt, and a couple turns of pepper. Form into 4 patties and dredge in the bread crumbs on the plate, turning to coat both sides.

FRY THE FISH CAKES: Heat a large heavy skillet over medium heat. When hot, pour in 3 tablespoons of the oil. Add the fish cakes and cook, turning once, until golden and cooked through, 8 to 10 minutes.

SERVE: Halve the lemon and squeeze half of the juice into a bowl. Cut the other half into wedges. Toss the baby greens with the lemon juice and remaining 2 tablespoons oil. Season with ½ teaspoon salt and a couple turns of pepper. Serve the fish cakes with the salad and lemon wedges on the side.

SERVES 4

ACTIVE TIME

15 minutes

TOTAL TIME

25 minutes

If you don't have a gas stove, wrap a stack of **TORTILLAS** in a clean dish towel and steam them for 5 minutes, or heat in the microwave for 1 to 2 minutes.

MARINATED TILAPIA TACOS

Salpicón—cold chopped vegetables, meat, or fish—is a traditional Latin appetizer. Here, it becomes an easy make-ahead taco filling, perfect for hot weather. Toasting tortillas directly over a hot burner means one less pan to wash.

1½ pounds skinless **tilapia fillets**

Kosher salt and freshly ground **black pepper**

2 tablespoons **extra-virgin olive oil**

¼ cup fresh **lime juice** (about 4 limes), plus wedges for serving

2 tablespoons **Worcestershire sauce**

½ cup loosely packed fresh **cilantro leaves**

1 **jalapeño pepper**, seeded and finely chopped

½ **red onion**, thinly sliced

8 to 12 (6-inch) **corn tortillas**

½ cup shredded **iceberg lettuce**

Sour cream and **hot sauce**, for serving

COOK THE FISH: Sprinkle the fish with ½ teaspoon salt and a couple turns of pepper. Heat a large skillet over high heat. When hot, pour in the oil. Sear the fish, turning once, until golden and cooked through, about 8 minutes. Let the fish cool to warm, then shred with a fork. Toss the fish with the oil from the skillet, the lime juice, Worcestershire, cilantro, jalapeño, onion, 1 teaspoon salt, and a couple turns of pepper. Cover and refrigerate until ready to use, or for up to 8 hours.

TOAST THE TORTILLAS: Use tongs to hold the tortillas directly over medium heat, turning once, until blackened in spots, about 30 seconds per side. Stack the tortillas as you go and cover with a kitchen towel.

SERVE: Put out the salpicón with the tortillas, lettuce, lime wedges, and sour cream and hot sauce so everyone can make their own tacos.

SERVES 4

ACTIVE TIME

10 minutes

TOTAL TIME

25 minutes

Q:

WHAT IS YOUR
MOST OFF-
THE-BEATEN-
PATH PANTRY
INGREDIENT?

A:

"I always have a
tube of harissa in
my fridge. I love
that flavor and it
changes a dish
instantly when you
add just a little."

**—JUDGE AMANDA
FREITAG**

MOROCCAN SPICE BLACKENED CATFISH

Warm North African seasoning adds toasty spice to a classic Southern fish preparation. The carrot salad on page 123 is the perfect foil for its flavors.

1 tablespoon plus 1 teaspoon ground **coriander**

2 teaspoons ground **cumin**

1 teaspoon **Chinese five-spice powder**

½ teaspoon **cayenne**

Kosher salt and freshly ground **black pepper**

4 (10- to 12-ounce) skinless **catfish fillets**

½ cup **mayonnaise**

2 teaspoons **harissa**

1 teaspoon grated **lemon zest**

1½ teaspoons fresh **lemon juice**

¼ cup **extra-virgin olive oil**

SEASON THE FISH: Stir together the coriander, cumin, five-spice, cayenne, 2 teaspoons salt, and a couple turns of pepper. Rub the spice blend all over the catfish.

MAKE THE HARISSA MAYO: Stir together the mayonnaise, harissa, lemon zest, lemon juice, and ¼ teaspoon salt and a couple turns of pepper.

SAUTÉ THE CATFISH: Heat a heavy skillet over medium-high heat. When hot, pour in 2 tablespoons of the oil. Sauté 2 of the catfish fillets, flipping once, halfway through, until well browned and cooked through, 8 to 10 minutes. Repeat with the remaining oil and catfish fillets.

SERVE: Put the catfish on plates with a dollop of the harissa mayo.

ARCTIC CHAR

WONTON WRAPPERS

MARKET BASKET

We hear from viewers that an unfamiliar fish can be a little intimidating. Arctic char may be new to you, but just think of it as a milder, smaller salmon. All you really need for it is salt and pepper, but if you're up for a *Chopped*-style challenge, corn, watercress, and wonton wrappers turn it into a party.

EACH RECIPE SERVES 4

CREAMED CORN

WATERCRESS

CORN RAVIOLI WITH CRESS PESTO AND CHAR

Rinse and drain two 14-ounce cans **creamed corn.** Stir with ½ cup each **ricotta** and grated **Parmesan,** a couple turns freshly ground **black pepper,** and ½ teaspoon **kosher salt.** Fill 32 **wonton wrappers** with 2 teaspoons each of corn filling. Wet the edges and fold into triangular ravioli. Pulse 2 cups **watercress** in a food processor with ¼ cup toasted **pine nuts,** ¼ cup grated **Parmesan,** 2 teaspoons fresh **lemon juice,** ½ teaspoon salt, and some pepper. Drizzle in 2 tablespoons **extra-virgin olive oil.** Sprinkle two 6-ounce skinless **arctic char** fillets with salt and pepper, then sear in 2 tablespoons extra-virgin olive oil in a skillet over high heat, flipping once, until just cooked through, about 3 minutes total. Boil the ravioli in salted water until tender, about 4 minutes. Drain, reserving ¼ cup cooking water. Whisk the water into the pesto, then toss with the pasta. Flake the char over the top and serve with shaved Parmesan. TOTAL TIME: 1 HOUR

CHAR-CORN-CRESS CHOWDER WITH WONTON CRACKERS

Brush 4 **wonton wrappers** with 2 tablespoons **vegetable oil** and sprinkle with a pinch each of **kosher salt** and freshly ground **black pepper.** Cut into triangles. Bake the wontons on a baking sheet at 450°F until golden and crisp, about 6 minutes. Cook 1 chopped **onion** in 2 tablespoons **unsalted butter** in a skillet over medium heat until softened, about 6 minutes. Stir in 1 tablespoon **all-purpose flour** and ¾ teaspoon kosher salt and a couple turns of pepper. Whisk 3 cups **whole milk** into the onion and bring to a boil. Stir in one 14-ounce can **creamed corn.** Return to a boil, then remove from the heat. Stir in 12 ounces skinless **arctic char** cut into 1-inch cubes and 2 cups chopped **watercress** and let sit until the fish is just cooked through, about 8 minutes. Serve with the wonton crackers. TOTAL TIME: 45 MINUTES

CHAR NOODLE CASSEROLE WITH CRESS SALAD

Sauté 1 chopped **onion** in 2 tablespoons **unsalted butter** in a large ovenproof skillet over medium heat until browned, then sprinkle with 3 tablespoons **all-purpose flour.** Whisk in 2 cups **chicken broth,** 1½ cups **milk,** and one 14-ounce can **creamed corn** and bring to a boil, whisking. Cut 10 **wonton wrappers** into matchsticks and add to the sauce. Simmer, stirring, for 10 minutes. Remove from the heat and stir in 9 ounces skinless **arctic char** cut into 1-inch pieces. Sprinkle the casserole with 1½ cups shredded **Cheddar** and ¼ cup **panko bread crumbs.** Broil 6 inches from the heat until golden, about 3 minutes. Toss 4 cups torn **watercress** with 1 tablespoon **extra-virgin olive oil,** 2 teaspoons **cider vinegar,** and **kosher salt** and **black pepper** to taste. Serve with the casserole. TOTAL TIME: 45 MINUTES

SLOW-COOKED SALMON
WITH OLIVE-BREAD CRUMB SPRINKLE

Slow-roasting salmon brings out its creamy texture (and makes it easy to cook perfectly), which is complemented by crunchy, crispy-briny olive crumbs.

Extra-virgin olive oil, for the dish
1 medium **zucchini**
1 tablespoon fresh **lemon juice** (about ½ lemon)
Kosher salt and freshly ground **black pepper**
1 (2-pound) center-cut **salmon fillet** (preferably wild), with skin
1 teaspoon grated **lemon zest**
2 tablespoons **unsalted butter**, melted
3 tablespoons finely chopped **kalamata olives** (about 10 olives)
1 teaspoon finely chopped fresh **thyme**
½ cup **panko bread crumbs**

SET UP: Preheat the oven to 250°F. Oil a 5-quart baking dish.

MARINATE THE ZUCCHINI: Thinly slice the zucchini into rounds. Toss with the lemon juice and ½ teaspoon salt and a couple turns of pepper. Layer the zucchini in the prepared dish, slightly overlapping the slices; the zucchini should just cover the bottom of the dish.

PREP THE SALMON: Rub the salmon with the lemon zest, ¾ teaspoon salt, and a couple turns of pepper. Put the salmon on top of the zucchini, skin-side down. Stir together the butter, olives, and thyme and spread over the salmon. Sprinkle the panko over the olives.

COOK THE SALMON: Bake the salmon until it's firm and just cooked through, 25 to 30 minutes. Turn the broiler to high and broil the salmon 2 to 3 inches from the heat until the panko is browned, about 1 minute.

SUPER-SAUCE GRILLED SALMON WITH GRILLED SCALLIONS

This fridge-door glaze comes together in minutes, and it's good on everything—save leftover sauce for grilled chicken, steamed shrimp, or even dumplings..

¼ cup **ketchup**

2 tablespoons **pure maple syrup**

1 tablespoon **hot sauce**

1 tablespoon **soy sauce**

1 tablespoon **balsamic vinegar**

1 **garlic clove**

Kosher salt

4 (6-ounce) **salmon steaks** (preferably wild)

Freshly ground **black pepper**

3 bunches **scallions**

1 tablespoon **extra-virgin olive oil**

SET UP: Prepare a grill or a grill pan, heat to medium-high heat, and lightly oil the grates.

MAKE THE SUPER SAUCE: Stir together the ketchup, maple syrup, hot sauce, soy sauce, and vinegar. Using a chef's knife, mash the garlic to a paste with ¼ teaspoon salt and stir into the sauce.

GRILL THE SALMON AND SCALLIONS: Lightly sprinkle the salmon with salt and pepper. Brush some of the sauce on the salmon. Grill, flipping once and brushing the salmon with the remaining sauce, until the fish is just cooked through, about 6 minutes. Toss the scallions with the oil and ¼ teaspoon salt and a couple turns of pepper. Grill, flipping once, until charred and slightly wilted, 1 to 2 minutes. Serve the salmon with the scallions.

SERVES 4

ACTIVE TIME

10 minutes

TOTAL TIME

20 minutes

When you buy
MUSSELS, pull off
the beards before
cooking and give
them a quick rinse.
Throw out any
mussels that are
open *before* cook-
ing (and don't close
when you tap them)
as well as any that
haven't opened *after*
cooking.

ALMOND AND WHITE WINE MUSSELS

The sunny Spanish-style garnish of toasted almonds, paprika, and
parsley brightens up each bite of these brothy, briny shellfish.

½ cup **almonds**
¾ cup packed fresh **flat-leaf parsley leaves**
½ teaspoon **smoked sweet paprika**
6 tablespoons (¾ stick) **unsalted butter**
5 **garlic cloves**, thinly sliced
Freshly ground **black pepper**
1 cup **white wine**
3 pounds **mussels**, rinsed
Crusty bread and **lemon wedges**, for serving

SET UP: Preheat the oven to 350°F.

TOAST THE NUTS: Spread the nuts on a baking sheet and toast until
fragrant and golden, 7 to 10 minutes. Check frequently, as they can burn
quickly. Cool before using.

MAKE THE ALMOND TOPPING: Pulse the almonds, the parsley, and
the paprika in a food processor until evenly chopped.

STEAM THE MUSSELS: Melt the butter in a large heavy pot over
medium-high heat. Stir in the garlic and a couple turns of pepper and
cook, stirring, until golden, about 3 minutes. Stir in the wine and bring
to a boil. Add the mussels and cover the pot. Cook, shaking the pot
occasionally, until the mussels have opened wide, 6 to 8 minutes. Reserve
¼ cup of the almond topping for garnish; sprinkle the remaining topping
over the mussels and stir to combine.

SERVE: Divide the mussels among 4 serving bowls and sprinkle with
the reserved almond topping. Serve with crusty bread and lemon wedges.

BROILED TROUT WITH NEW ORLEANS BROWN BUTTER SAUCE

Cream sauce and fish sauce together? We were doubtful, but classic creamy mushroom sauce gets lively brightness from fish sauce and cilantro in this tribute to New Orleans's Vietnamese community.

4 tablespoons (½ stick) **unsalted butter**

8 ounces **white mushrooms**, halved or quartered if large (about 3 cups)

1 small **green bell pepper**, chopped

1 **shallot**, sliced

Kosher salt and freshly ground **black pepper**

½ cup **white wine**

½ cup **chicken broth**

1 tablespoon **Asian fish sauce**

¼ cup **heavy cream**

1 teaspoon **cornstarch**

1 teaspoon **hot sauce**

4 (4-ounce) skin-on **trout fillets**, pin bones removed

¼ cup loosely packed fresh **cilantro leaves**

SET UP: Preheat the broiler with a rack set 2 inches away from the heat source.

MAKE THE SAUCE: Heat 2 tablespoons of the butter in a heavy skillet over medium heat. Stir in the mushrooms, bell pepper, shallot, ½ teaspoon salt, and a couple turns of pepper. Cook, covered, until the mushrooms release their liquid, about 4 minutes. Uncover and cook until the vegetables are pale golden, about 5 minutes more. Add the wine and boil until reduced to a glaze, about 8 minutes. Add the broth and fish sauce and boil until reduced by half, about 4 minutes. Stir together the cream and cornstarch, and stir into the sauce. Simmer until thickened, about 1 minute. Stir in the hot sauce.

BROIL THE TROUT: Melt the remaining 2 tablespoons butter. Put the trout skin-side up on a rimmed baking sheet and spoon the butter over the top. Sprinkle with salt and pepper and broil until just cooked through, about 2 minutes.

SERVE: Transfer the trout to serving plates. Spoon the sauce over the top and sprinkle with the cilantro.

This flavor-packed sauce is remarkably versatile: We especially love it in place of hollandaise on our **eggs Benedict.** Flake the cooked **trout** onto well-toasted **English muffins** and top with poached eggs and the sauce, or skip the trout altogether and use the traditional ham. (To poach an egg, crack it into a ramekin, then slide it into a saucepan of barely simmering water with a splash of vinegar added. After 3 to 5 minutes, scoop it out with a slotted spoon and drain on paper towels.)

BIG
EASY
BENEDICT

SHIITAKE stems are pretty tough; trim them before using and save them to add flavor to stocks or broths.

SHRIMP RAMEN

Ramen noodles (yes, the ones from the package) can be dressed up with poached shrimp and bacon to make a porky, smoky broth that tastes slow-simmered.

8 ounces **bacon**, chopped

5 **garlic cloves**, thinly sliced

2 cups sliced stemmed **shiitake mushrooms** (about 6 ounces)

7 cups **chicken broth**

1 teaspoon **soy sauce**

1 teaspoon **Worcestershire sauce**

2 (3-ounce) packages **ramen noodles**, flavor packets discarded

12 ounces peeled and deveined medium **shrimp**, halved lengthwise (about 20 shrimp)

2 tablespoons 1-inch-long pieces **chives**

COOK THE AROMATICS: Put the bacon in a cold medium saucepan and cook over medium-high heat, stirring occasionally, until golden, about 6 minutes. Remove all but 3 tablespoons of the bacon fat from the pan. Stir in the garlic and cook until golden, about 3 minutes. Stir in the shiitakes and cook until well browned, about 6 minutes more.

MAKE THE BROTH: Stir in the chicken broth, soy sauce, and Worcestershire and bring to a boil. Stir in the ramen noodles and boil until tender, about 2 minutes.

ADD THE SHRIMP AND SERVE: Remove the broth from the heat and stir in the shrimp. Let stand until the shrimp are cooked, 1 to 2 minutes. Serve topped with the chives.

Q:

WHAT IS ALWAYS IN YOUR FREEZER?

A:

"I always keep wild-caught Gulf shrimp in my freezer for a quick and easy dinner."

—JUDGE AARON SANCHEZ

CONNECTICUT-CAJUN
SHRIMP ROLLS

Poaching shell-on shrimp in flavorful broth intensifies their sweet, briny flavor for these buttery sandwiches. If you can find New England–style split-top hot dog buns, use them; they have extra surface area for browning, making for a super-crisp contrast to the tender shrimp. Save the broth to use as a base for fish chowder or stew.

4 medium **carrots**, chopped

2 **celery stalks**, chopped

1 head of **garlic**, halved crosswise

1 tablespoon **black peppercorns**

5 **bay leaves**

5 sprigs of fresh **thyme**

1 tablespoon plus 1 teaspoon **Cajun seasoning**

1 cup **red wine vinegar**

Kosher salt

1 pound medium **shrimp**, in the shells

6 tablespoons (¾ stick) **unsalted butter**

4 split-top or regular **hot dog buns**

2 tablespoons minced fresh **chives**

Lettuce leaves, for serving

MAKE THE POACHING LIQUID: Put the carrots, celery, garlic, peppercorns, bay leaves, thyme, 1 tablespoon of the Cajun seasoning, the vinegar, and 1 teaspoon salt in a medium pot and cover with 6 cups water. Bring to a boil over high heat, then reduce the heat and simmer for about 15 minutes. Scoop out the solids with a strainer and discard (or save the bigger veggies for adding to salads), reserving the poaching liquid.

POACH THE SHRIMP: Bring the poaching liquid back to a simmer and stir in the shrimp. Poach until the shrimp are just cooked through, about 2 minutes. Use a slotted spoon to transfer the shrimp to a plate and then refrigerate until cool enough to handle. Peel and devein the shrimp and coarsely chop.

TOAST THE BUNS: Melt the butter and remaining 1 teaspoon Cajun seasoning in a large skillet over medium heat. Brush the cut sides of the buns with some of the butter and toast in the skillet, buttered side down, until golden, a minute or two.

SERVE: Toss the shrimp with the chives and season with salt. Divide the lettuce and shrimp among the buns, drizzling with any remaining butter. Serve immediately.

GREAT
GRAINS

Grains are a fantastic food to have on hand—they keep forever in the freezer (truly the best place to store them to ensure freshness) and make for a filling, comforting dinner when you're short on ingredients. Check our guide to cook times on pages 201–203.

THREE-ONION FARRO SOUP

CHEDDAR-BARLEY CASSEROLE

GO-TO GUIDE: COOKING GRAINS

QUINOA SHRIMP FRIED "RICE"

BULGUR VEGETABLE PILAF

OAT AND WHOLE-GRAIN BISCUITS

STUFFED PEPPERS WITH WHEAT BERRIES

CARROT AND ALMOND ARANCINI

ROASTED CARROT AND ONION RISOTTO

CHORIZO AND CHICKEN
BROWN RICE PAELLA

MUSHROOM AND CHEESE BAKED POLENTA

THREE-ONION FARRO SOUP

Farro takes this classic soup from a starter to a filling meal. Pearled or quick-cooking farro cooks to nutty-tender and satisfying.

4 tablespoons (½ stick) **unsalted butter**

2 medium **leeks** (white and tender green parts), sliced into half-moons, washed

2 large **onions,** sliced

1 bunch **scallions**, sliced, 2 tablespoons of the greens reserved

Kosher salt and freshly ground **black pepper**

1 cup pearled or quick-cooking **farro**

½ cup **white wine**

4 cups **chicken broth**

2 cups **beef broth**

1 tablespoon **Worcestershire sauce**

2 fresh or dried **bay leaves**

1 cup grated **Gruyère** (about 4 ounces)

CARAMELIZE THE ONIONS: Melt the butter in a Dutch oven over medium heat. Add the leeks, onions, scallion whites, 1½ teaspoons salt, and a couple turns of pepper. Cover and cook, stirring every 4 or 5 minutes, until the onion is very soft, about 15 minutes. Uncover, increase the heat to medium-high, and cook, adjusting the heat as necessary and stirring often, until golden brown, 35 to 40 minutes more. (Loosen and scrape up any browned onion with a splash of water as necessary.)

SIMMER THE SOUP: Stir in the farro, add the wine, and bring to a boil, scraping up any brown bits off the bottom of the pan. Add the chicken and beef broths, 2 cups water, the Worcestershire, and bay leaves, and bring to a boil. Reduce the heat so the soup simmers, and cook until the farro is tender, about 15 minutes. Discard the bay leaves.

SET UP: Preheat the broiler to high with a rack set 4 inches from the heat source.

BROIL THE CHEESE: Divide the soup among flame-proof serving bowls and sprinkle with the Gruyère. Broil 4 inches from the heat until the cheese is golden, 3 to 4 minutes. Sprinkle with the reserved scallion greens and serve.

CHEDDAR-BARLEY CASSEROLE

Barley adds nutty whole-grain chew to the ultimate comfort food in this mac-and-cheese-esque decadent side dish or elegant main course.

2 tablespoons **unsalted butter**, plus more for the baking dish

3 slices **bacon**, cut into 1-inch pieces

2 **garlic cloves**, minced

1 medium **onion**, chopped

1 cup **pearl barley**

Kosher salt and freshly ground **black pepper**

2½ cups **chicken broth**

½ cup **heavy cream**

1 cup grated **Cheddar** (about 4 ounces)

SET UP: Preheat the oven to 375°F. Butter a 1½-quart baking dish.

PREPARE THE CASSEROLE: Put the bacon in a cold skillet and cook over medium heat until crisp, about 7 minutes, stirring occasionally. Transfer the bacon to a paper-towel-lined plate to drain. Melt the butter in the same skillet with the bacon fat. Add the garlic and onion and cook until translucent, about 3 minutes. Add the barley and cook, stirring, until it begins to brown, about 3 minutes. Season with ½ teaspoon salt and a couple turns of pepper. Stir in the chicken broth and heavy cream. Bring to a boil and cook until the liquid begins to thicken slightly, about 2 minutes. Stir in the bacon and ¾ cup of the Cheddar. Pour into the prepared baking dish. Cover tightly with foil.

BAKE THE CASSEROLE: Bake the casserole until the barley is bubbling, about 25 minutes. Remove the foil, stir, and sprinkle with the remaining ¼ cup cheese. Return to the oven and cook, uncovered, until the cheese is melted and most of the liquid is absorbed, 10 to 15 minutes. Let sit for a few minutes before serving.

COOKING GRAINS

THERE ARE SEVERAL WAYS to cook grains perfectly tender-toothsome every time. We most often rely on these four methods, using water, broth, or a combination of the two.

RICE STYLE: This is the back-of-the-box classic way to cook grains. Bring **liquid** to a boil. Add **grain** and **salt,** bring to a simmer, stir once, cover, and simmer until the liquid is absorbed. Let sit off the heat for 5 minutes, undisturbed, before serving.

PILAF STYLE: This style adds nuttiness and helps keep grains from sticking together. Gently toast the **grain** in the pan in a small amount of **fat** before adding the **liquid.** Stir in the liquid and **salt,** cover, and simmer. Then let sit off the heat for 5 minutes before fluffing with a fork.

PASTA STYLE: This is an easy, foolproof method—you don't even need to measure anything, and it works for almost every grain. Add the **grain** to lots of boiling **salted water** and cook until tender, then drain.

RISOTTO STYLE: This style makes a great, creamy dish—but you have to tend it the whole time. Arborio rice, farro, and pearled barley all work great with this method. Heat a couple tablespoons **butter** or **olive oil** in a saucepan. Add **aromatics** (onions/shallots/garlic) and cook until translucent. Add the **grain** and stir to coat in the fat. Add a splash of **wine** (white, red, or fortified) and cook, stirring, until absorbed. Then add ½ cup of **broth** at a time, stirring until the liquid is absorbed before adding more, until the grain is tender and creamy. Finish with **grated cheese** if desired.

Finish as desired with a pat of butter, a swirl of olive oil, or a dusting of fresh herbs or grated cheese.

(continued)

(continued from page 201)

GRAIN	GO-TO METHOD
BARLEY Pearl barley is the most common type. The hull is removed and the grain is then polished. Cooked barley is chewy and nutty.	Bring 3 cups **water** to a boil. Add ½ teaspoon **kosher salt** and 1 cup **barley** and bring back to a boil. Cover and cook until tender, about 45 minutes. Fluff with a fork. (Pearl barley can also be cooked directly in soup and stews; it absorbs lots of liquid, though, so make sure you have enough. Quick barley is done in about 15 minutes, and is great for weeknights.)
BULGUR Bulgur is whole wheat that has been parcooked, dried, and ground. There are several grinds, from fine to coarse. We find medium the most versatile.	Bring 2 cups **water** to a boil. Season with ½ teaspoon **kosher salt**. Add 1 cup **medium-grind bulgur**, cover, and remove from the heat. Let sit for 20 to 25 minutes until the bulgur is tender. (This soaking method gives a chewy texture that is perfect for salads. Bulgur can also be cooked using the pasta method, but we find this to be the easiest way.)
FARRO Farro is an ancient type of wheat. It is available regular or pearled and semi-pearled, which have portions of the hull removed. We like semi-pearled, as it has more nutrition than pearled, but takes less time to cook than regular.	Add 1 cup farro to plenty of boiling, **salted water**. Boil for about 40 minutes for regular farro, and about 20 minutes for semi-pearled and pearled. Drain. (You can also cook farro risotto style.)
MILLET Millet is used in breads, soups, and stews and to make porridge. Toasting the millet in a pan before cooking helps the grains stay firm instead of turning mushy and adds a delicious nuttiness.	Heat a saucepan over medium heat. Add 2 teaspoons **olive oil** and 1 cup **millet** and cook the millet, stirring, until coated and light brown, about 5 minutes. Add 2 cups **water** and ½ teaspoon **kosher salt** and bring to a simmer. Cover and cook for 15 minutes. Remove from heat and let stand, covered, for 10 minutes. Fluff with a fork.
POLENTA/YELLOW CORNMEAL Polenta is ground yellow or white corn. Many assume polenta and grits are the same, but grits are ground hominy (hominy is corn that has been processed to remove its outer hull). Quick-cooking polenta has a creamier texture and cooks in 5 to 15 minutes instead of 45.	Bring 5 cups **liquid** to a boil, then gently whisk in 1 cup **polenta**, stirring to remove lumps. Over low heat, continue to cook, stirring frequently, until the polenta is thick, creamy, and pulling away from the side of the pot, about 45 minutes. (You can add cheese and/or butter at the end for more flavor.)
QUINOA Quinoa is actually a seed, but can be cooked like a whole grain. It should be rinsed before cooking or it can be bitter.	Rinse well before cooking. Combine 1 cup **quinoa** with 2½ to 3 cups **water** (depending on how soft you want the final result) and ½ teaspoon **kosher salt** in a saucepan. Bring to a boil, reduce the heat so the water simmers, and cook, uncovered, until tender, about 15 minutes.

GRAIN	GO-TO METHOD
ARBORIO RICE Arborio rice is a short-grain rice with a higher-than-usual starch content, which is what gives risotto its creaminess. Vialone nano and carnaroli are similar options—both make a slightly creamier, quicker cooking, risotto	Heat 4 cups **broth** and reserve. Heat 1 to 2 tablespoons **extra-virgin olive oil** in a saucepan over medium heat. Add ½ finely chopped **onion** and cook, stirring, until translucent, 4 minutes. Add 1 cup **Arborio rice** and cook, stirring, until the rice is glossy, 1 minute. Add ½ cup warm broth and stir constantly until absorbed. Repeat, adding the broth in ½ cup increments and stirring constantly, until the liquid is absorbed and the rice is creamy and just tender, 20 to 25 minutes. Season with **salt** and **pepper.** Remove from the heat. (You can add cheese, cooked veggies, and/or a little butter at the end for more flavor.)
BASMATI RICE Basmati is a long-grain rice most commonly used in India and the Middle East. It is one of thousands of types of rice and can be found both brown and white. We like basmati rice for its flavor—basmati is nuttier and more fragrant than typical white rice. Instructions here are for white basmati rice. Brown basmati is great when cooked like pasta.	Rinse 1 cup **basmati rice** until the water runs clear. Combine the rice, 1¾ cups **liquid**, and ½ teaspoon **kosher salt** in a saucepan. Bring to a boil over medium-high heat, cover, reduce the heat so the liquid simmers, and cook for about 15 minutes. Let stand for 5 minutes, covered. Fluff with a fork.
BROWN RICE Brown rice is whole-grain rice that has been processed only to remove the inedible outer hull. This is the most nutritious type of rice. It takes longer to cook and has a chewier, nuttier flavor than white rice.	Rinse 1 cup **brown rice** well, then put in a saucepan with 2 cups **liquid**. Bring to a boil, reduce the heat so the liquid simmers, cover, and cook until the liquid is absorbed and the rice is tender, 45 to 50 minutes. Fluff the rice with a fork before serving.
WHITE RICE Rice is one of the most widely consumed cereal grains on the planet. It can range from sticky short-grained sushi rice to fluffy converted rice and floral-smelling jasmine rice to delicate basmati rice.	Melt 1 tablespoon **unsalted butter** in a saucepan over medium heat. Add 1½ cups **rice** and cook, stirring, until the rice is well coated and lightly toasted, about 2 minutes. Add 2¾ cups **broth** or **water** and ½ teaspoon **kosher salt** and bring to a simmer. Reduce the heat to medium-low, cover, and simmer until the water is absorbed, 18 minutes. Remove from the heat and let sit, covered, for 5 minutes. Uncover and fluff with a fork.
WHEAT BERRIES Wheat berries are whole-wheat kernels. Because they are the whole, complete grain and have not been processed at all, they take a little time to cook. Once cooked, they are nutty and slightly chewy. You can cook a big batch and freeze them.	Cover 1 cup **wheat berries** with plenty of **water**, bring to a boil, add **kosher salt**, and cook until tender, about 1 hour. Drain. (These are cooked like pasta—you don't need a measured amount of water, just enough so that the wheat berries can cook for an hour.)

QUINOA SHRIMP FRIED "RICE"

Quinoa stands in for rice, keeping the crisp texture of the traditional dish while adding protein. Fried eggs and their broken yolks turn into an unexpected creamy sauce. Those of us who like quinoa love this dish—and those of us who don't, like it just as much! If you have leftover cooked quinoa, use 2 cups of it here in place of raw.

1 cup **quinoa**

6 tablespoons **vegetable oil**

1 small **Japanese eggplant** (about 6 ounces), halved lengthwise and sliced crosswise ½ inch thick

1 small **carrot**, cut into thin matchsticks

1 bunch **scallions**, sliced (white and green parts kept separate)

2 **garlic cloves**, minced

1 (1-inch) piece fresh **ginger**, peeled and minced

2 tablespoons **soy sauce**

1 teaspoon **toasted sesame oil**

½ teaspoon **Asian fish sauce**

1 pound small **shrimp**, peeled and deveined

4 large **eggs**

Kosher salt

COOK THE QUINOA: Rinse the quinoa well. Bring the quinoa and 3 cups water to a boil in a large saucepan over high heat. Reduce the heat so the water simmers and cook until the quinoa is tender, about 15 minutes. Drain and spread on a rimmed baking sheet to cool.

MAKE THE QUINOA FRIED RICE: Heat 3 tablespoons of the vegetable oil in a large nonstick skillet or wok over medium-high heat. Add the eggplant and cook until it begins to brown, 2 to 3 minutes. Add 2 more tablespoons oil to the skillet and stir in the carrot, scallion whites, garlic, and ginger. Cook until the vegetables begin to soften, about 1 minute. Stir in the soy sauce, sesame oil, fish sauce, and shrimp. Cook, stirring, until the shrimp begin to change color, about 2 minutes. Add the cooled quinoa. Continue to cook, stirring, until the shrimp are fully cooked, about 3 minutes. Stir in half of the scallion greens. Divide the mixture among 4 shallow bowls.

FRY THE EGGS: Wipe out the skillet and heat the remaining tablespoon vegetable oil over medium-high heat. Crack the eggs into the skillet, sprinkle with a little salt, and cook until set, about 3 minutes.

SERVE: Top each bowl with a fried egg and scatter the remaining scallion greens over the top.

Q:

WHAT IS THE MOST MISUSED *CHOPPED* INGREDIENT?

A:

"Arugula! It often gets tossed in the mix as a way to tie many odd ingredients together. But arugula can be very distinctive. It can actually end up taking over and leaving other ingredients hidden."

—JUDGE ALEX GUARNASCHELLI

BULGUR VEGETABLE PILAF

Arugula is used as an herb in this spicy verdant pilaf made with bulgur wheat, which is super-flavorful and stands up to the sharp and peppery green. Serve with pita, hummus, and hard-boiled eggs for a complete meal.

½ cup **walnuts**, roughly chopped

3 tablespoons **extra-virgin olive oil**

½ medium **red onion**, diced

½ to 1 **chipotle chile in adobo**, to taste, chopped, plus 1 teaspoon adobo sauce

½ teaspoon ground **coriander**

Kosher salt and freshly ground **black pepper**

1 cup medium **bulgur**

1 cup **baby arugula**, chopped

1 cup frozen **green peas**, thawed

½ cup fresh **flat-leaf parsley leaves**, chopped

¼ cup chopped fresh **dill**

3 tablespoons **red wine vinegar**

SET UP: Preheat the oven to 350°F.

TOAST THE NUTS: Spread the nuts on a baking sheet and toast until fragrant and golden, 7 to 10 minutes. Check frequently, as they can burn quickly. Cool before using.

COOK THE BULGUR: Bring 2 cups water to a boil in a small saucepan. Heat 1 tablespoon of the oil in a medium saucepan over medium-high heat. Add the onion and cook until softened, about 2 minutes. Add the chipotle chile, adobo sauce, coriander, ½ teaspoon salt, and a couple turns of pepper. Cook, stirring, until fragrant, 1 minute. Add the bulgur and the boiling water. Cover, remove from the heat, and let stand until the bulgur is tender, about 25 minutes.

FINISH THE PILAF: Fluff the bulgur with a fork and pour into a large bowl. Toss in the arugula, green peas, parsley, dill, and walnuts. Stir in the remaining 2 tablespoons oil and the vinegar and season with salt and pepper. Serve at room temperature.

SERVES 6
(MAKES
ABOUT
FIFTEEN
2-INCH
BISCUITS)

ACTIVE TIME

10 minutes

TOTAL TIME

25 minutes

OAT AND WHOLE-GRAIN BISCUITS

Whole grains add nutty flavor, while biscuits stay tender and flaky thanks to careful folding. Serve as a side or on their own (filled with ham or jam).

1½ cups **whole-wheat pastry flour**, plus more for dusting

1 cup **old-fashioned rolled oats**

2 teaspoons **baking powder**

2 teaspoons **sugar**

Kosher salt and freshly ground **black pepper**

6 tablespoons (¾ stick) cold **unsalted butter**, cut into ¼-inch pieces

1 cup **buttermilk**, plus more for brushing

SET UP: Preheat the oven to 400°F. Line a rimmed baking sheet with parchment paper.

MIX THE DOUGH: Pulse the flour, oats, baking powder, sugar, 1 teaspoon salt, and ¼ teaspoon pepper in a food processor until the oats are finely ground. Add the butter and pulse until the mixture resembles a coarse meal. Pour into a large bowl and form a well in the center. Gently stir the buttermilk into the dough until it just comes together.

FORM THE BISCUITS: Turn the dough out onto a lightly floured surface. Flatten the dough into a rectangle about 1 inch thick. Fold the dough in thirds, like a letter. Flatten and repeat from the other direction. Roll or pat out to a generous ¾-inch thickness. Cut out using a 2- to 3-inch biscuit cutter, rerolling the scraps. Arrange on the prepared baking sheet, leaving 1½ to 2 inches between the biscuits. Brush the tops with buttermilk.

BAKE THE BISCUITS: Bake the biscuits until risen and light golden, 15 to 18 minutes. Serve warm or at room temperature.

SERVES 4

ACTIVE TIME

30 minutes

TOTAL TIME

1 hour
15 minutes

STUFFED PEPPERS
with **WHEAT BERRIES**

Creamy ricotta and a hint of peanut butter in the filling add richness without overpowering the flavor of the grains. Feel free to use 2 to 3 cups precooked brown rice and wheat berries in this great vegetarian dinner.

½ cup **brown rice**

½ cup **wheat berries**

Kosher salt

4 **orange bell peppers**, halved lengthwise and seeded

2 tablespoons **extra-virgin olive oil**, plus more for drizzling

1 **red jalapeño**, chopped

1 small **onion**, chopped

1 (14-ounce can) diced **tomatoes**, drained

Freshly ground **black pepper**

2 tablespoons smooth **peanut butter**

2 teaspoons **soy sauce**

1 cup **ricotta**

Nonstick cooking spray

¼ cup chopped **roasted peanuts**

COOK THE GRAINS: Combine the brown rice, wheat berries, 1 teaspoon salt, and 2¼ cups water in a large saucepan. Bring to a boil, reduce the heat, cover, and simmer until the wheat berries are tender, 45 to 50 minutes. Drain. The grains can be cooked in advance and kept in the fridge for up to 2 days.

SET UP: Preheat the oven to 375°F.

SOFTEN THE PEPPERS: Put the peppers in a large microwave-safe bowl and cover tightly with plastic wrap. Cook on high until the peppers begin to soften, about 6 minutes. Leave covered until ready to use. (Alternatively, put the peppers, cut-side down, in a 9 by 13-inch baking dish. Pour ¼ cup hot water into the dish, cover tightly with foil, and bake until the peppers just begin to soften, about 20 minutes. Leave covered until ready to use.)

(continued)

COOK THE FILLING: Heat the oil in a large skillet over medium-high heat. Add the jalapeño and onion and cook until soft, about 5 minutes. Add the tomatoes, 1 teaspoon salt, and a couple turns of pepper and cook until heated through, about 2 minutes. Stir in the peanut butter and soy sauce. Remove from the heat.

FILL THE PEPPERS: Combine the cooked grains, vegetables, ½ cup of the ricotta, and salt and pepper to taste. Divide the filling among the peppers and dot with the remaining ricotta. Spray a rimmed baking sheet and put the peppers on it. Drizzle with olive oil.

COOK THE PEPPERS: Bake until the tops are golden and the peppers are fully cooked, about 30 minutes. Sprinkle with the chopped peanuts and serve.

CARROT AND ALMOND ARANCINI

Leftover Roasted Carrot and Onion Risotto is put to good use in these Sicilian rice balls, but any flavor risotto works well. These make a filling vegetarian main dish (substitute vegetable for chicken stock in your risotto) or a nice appetizer for a dinner party.

½ cup slivered **almonds**

2 cups cold **Roasted Carrot and Onion Risotto** (page 212)

¼ cup loosely packed fresh **flat-leaf parsley leaves**, chopped

1 large **egg**

12 (½-inch) cubes **mozzarella** (about 2 ounces)

About 1 cup **panko bread crumbs**, for dredging

Extra-virgin olive oil, for shallow frying

2 cups **Quick and Easy Marinara** (page 27) or **Bell Pepper Marinara** (page 35), or store-bought marinara, warmed

SET UP: Preheat the oven to 350°F.

TOAST THE NUTS: Spread the nuts on a baking sheet and toast until fragrant and golden, 7 to 10 minutes. Check frequently, as they can burn quickly. Cool before using.

FORM THE RICE BALLS: Mix the risotto, almonds, parsley, and egg in a large bowl until well combined. Wrap about 2 tablespoons of the mixture around each cube of cheese, making 12 balls. Roll in the panko to coat, then freeze until just firm, about 10 minutes.

FRY THE RICE BALLS: Heat about ½ inch oil in a large deep skillet over medium heat until it reaches 350°F or a few pieces of rice bubble rapidly in the oil. Fry the rice balls in batches, turning occasionally, until golden brown on all sides and cooked through, about 6 minutes. Use a slotted spoon to transfer the balls to a paper-towel-lined plate. Serve with marinara for dipping.

ROASTED CARROT
AND ONION RISOTTO

Roasting carrots and onions coaxes out their sweetness, while ginger delivers refreshing bite. Save leftovers to make Carrot and Almond Arancini (page 211).

4 medium **carrots**, sliced on the diagonal

1 large **onion**, cut into ½-inch wedges

1 (2-inch) piece fresh **ginger**, peeled and minced

¼ cup **vegetable oil**

Kosher salt and freshly ground **black pepper**

4 cups **chicken broth**

1½ cups **Arborio rice**

½ cup **white wine**

2 sprigs of fresh **thyme**

3 tablespoons cold **unsalted butter**, cubed

SET UP: Preheat the oven to 400°F.

ROAST THE VEGETABLES: Toss the carrots, onion, and ginger with 2 tablespoons of the oil, 1 teaspoon salt, and a couple turns of pepper on a baking sheet. Roast until the vegetables are tender and lightly browned, about 20 minutes.

MAKE THE RISOTTO: Meanwhile, heat the chicken broth with 3 cups water in a medium saucepan over medium heat; keep it just under a simmer. Heat the remaining 2 tablespoons oil in another medium saucepan over medium heat. Add the rice and cook, stirring, until the rice is translucent, about 1 minute. Add the wine and simmer, stirring, until the wine is fully absorbed, about 2 minutes. Add the thyme sprigs and season with ½ teaspoon salt and a couple turns of pepper. Add about ½ cup warm broth. Cook, stirring, until the broth is almost absorbed. Continue adding broth, ½ cup at a time, and stirring until all of the broth has been incorporated and the rice is tender, but not mushy, about 25 minutes total. Stir in the butter, a few cubes at a time, until they are melted and the risotto is creamy.

SERVE: Roughly chop half of the roasted vegetables and stir them into the risotto. Spoon into bowls and garnish with the remaining vegetables.

SERVES 4

ACTIVE TIME

30 minutes

TOTAL TIME

1 hour
30 minutes

If you love **CHICKEN SKIN,** leave it on and start it skin side down, then turn it skin side up when you nestle it into the rice.

CHORIZO AND CHICKEN BROWN RICE PAELLA

This streamlined paella makes use of long-grain basmati brown rice (as a substitute for the traditional, but harder to find, bomba rice), which adds nuttiness to the dish and turns into a fine accompaniment for the flavors of Spain.

1 tablespoon **extra-virgin olive oil**

4 ounces **Spanish chorizo**, peeled and cut into thin half-moons

4 bone-in **chicken thighs** (about 14 ounces), skin removed

Kosher salt and freshly ground **black pepper**

1 medium **onion**, chopped

1 **red bell pepper**, chopped

¼ teaspoon **saffron** (optional)

½ cup **white wine**

2 cups **chicken broth**

1½ cups **brown basmati rice**

1 tablespoon **tomato paste**

1 medium **tomato**, chopped

1 cup frozen **green peas**, thawed

BROWN THE CHORIZO AND CHICKEN: Heat a large deep skillet over medium-high heat. When hot, pour in the oil. Add the chorizo and cook, stirring, until the chorizo is golden brown and has rendered some of its fat, about 3 minutes. Using a slotted spoon, transfer the chorizo to a plate. Sprinkle the chicken with salt and pepper. Add the chicken to the fat in the skillet and cook, turning once, until golden brown on both sides, about 6 minutes total. Transfer the chicken to the plate with the chorizo.

MAKE THE PAELLA: Add the onion and bell pepper to the skillet and cook until golden, about 8 minutes. Stir in the saffron if using, followed by the wine, and boil until reduced by half, about 1 minute. Add the chicken broth, rice, tomato paste, and tomato. Bring to a full boil over high heat and boil for 1 minute. Nestle the chicken into the rice and scatter the chorizo over the top. Reduce the heat to low and cover the

skillet tightly with foil and a lid. Simmer until the rice is tender and the liquid has been absorbed, about 50 minutes.

FINISH THE PAELLA: Remove the lid and scatter the peas over the top. Increase the heat to medium-high and re-cover, steaming the peas and letting a crust form on the bottom of the skillet, about 5 minutes. Serve straight from the skillet.

SERVES 4 AS A
MAIN DISH OR
8 AS A SIDE

ACTIVE TIME

30 minutes

TOTAL TIME

1 hour

If you have **DRIED PORCINI MUSH-ROOMS,** this is the place to use them—up to half an ounce would add incredible earthy depth to this bake. Rehydrate them in 1½ cups hot water before adding—strain and reserve the liquid for soups or sauces.

MUSHROOM AND CHEESE
BAKED POLENTA

Polenta meets spoonbread, without the stirring. This simple batter puffs up creamy and rich with the help of whipped egg whites.

> 4 tablespoons (½ stick) **unsalted butter**, plus more for the baking dish
> 1 pound mixed **mushrooms**, such as cremini, porcini, or stemmed sliced shiitakes
> **Kosher salt** and freshly ground **black pepper**
> 2 cups **milk**
> ½ cup **heavy cream**
> 1 cup **polenta**
> 2 teaspoons **sugar**
> ½ teaspoon **baking powder**
> 3 large **eggs**, separated
> 1 cup shredded white **Cheddar** (about 4 ounces)

SET UP: Preheat the oven to 375°F. Butter a 2-quart baking dish.

SAUTÉ THE MUSHROOMS: Melt the butter in a large pot over medium heat. Add the mushrooms, 1 teaspoon salt, and a couple turns of pepper and cook until the mushrooms are tender, about 4 minutes. Add the milk and heavy cream and heat until very warm.

ADD THE POLENTA: Whisk the polenta, sugar, baking powder, 1 teaspoon salt, and a couple turns of pepper in a large bowl. Whisk the mushroom sauce into the polenta until well combined and thick. Whisk the egg yolks in a small bowl. Whisk ½ cup of the hot polenta into the yolks, repeat twice, then pour the yolk mixture into the remaining polenta. Stir in the Cheddar.

BEAT THE EGG WHITES: Whip the egg whites with a pinch of salt until soft, glossy peaks form. Fold the egg whites into the polenta mixture in three additions.

BAKE THE CASSEROLE: Spoon the polenta into the prepared baking dish. Bake until golden and puffed, 25 to 30 minutes. Serve immediately.

SHORT AND SWEET EASY DESSERTS

Here are ten quick and easy desserts using ingredients you probably already have at home—and not a single French toast among them.

MELTED ICE CREAM CHOCOLATE MOUSSE

BLACK FOREST DESSERT PIZZA

WARM SALTED CARAMEL BANANA
PUDDING

THIN LEMON PANCAKES WITH SWEETENED
SOUR CREAM AND BLUEBERRIES

CHILE AFFOGATO

MOCHA BROWNIES WITH COFFEE
AND CINNAMON

MARKET BASKET: STRAWBERRIES

COCONUT PANNA COTTA
WITH CANDIED PEANUTS

SERVES 4

ACTIVE TIME

20 minutes

TOTAL TIME

2 hours

MELTED ICE CREAM
CHOCOLATE MOUSSE

Melted ice cream is the base of this decadent dessert, which comes together quickly but tastes like it took all day to make. Whip your whites before the cream; a scrupulously clean whisk helps whites fluff up nicely.

1 cup melted premium **vanilla ice cream**

1 tablespoon unsweetened **cocoa powder**, sifted

6 ounces chopped 70% **bittersweet chocolate**, plus 2 tablespoons shaved

3 large pasteurized **egg whites**

Kosher salt

½ cup **heavy cream**

MAKE THE CHOCOLATE BASE: Whisk the ice cream and cocoa powder in a saucepan, making sure there are no lumps. Heat over medium heat until simmering. Put the chopped chocolate in a bowl and pour the heated ice cream over the top. Stir to evenly melt the chocolate, then let cool to warm.

WHIP THE EGG WHITES: Beat the egg whites with a pinch of salt until they hold stiff peaks. Whisk one-third of the whites into the chocolate base to lighten. Gently fold in the remaining egg whites.

FINISH THE MOUSSE: Beat the cream until it just holds medium-stiff peaks, then fold into the mousse. Divide the mousse among 4 serving bowls and chill until set, about 1½ hours. Serve topped with the shaved chocolate.

If you have frozen **STRAWBERRIES** on hand, those work great here; swap out some or all of the chocolate chips for peanut butter chips for a PB&J pie.

BLACK FOREST
DESSERT PIZZA

Pizza lovers, rejoice. You can have it for dessert, too! Sweet-tart cherries, melted chocolate, and whipped cream step out of cake and onto sugared dough to deliver amazing flavor in this handheld treat.

- ¼ cup plus 2 tablespoons **sugar**
- 2 cups frozen **pitted cherries**, thawed
- ¼ teaspoon **almond extract**
- 2 teaspoons fresh **lemon juice**
- 8 ounces frozen **pizza dough**, thawed and at room temperature
- 1 tablespoon **unsalted butter**, melted
- ½ cup **semisweet chocolate chips**
- ½ cup **heavy cream**

SET UP: Preheat the oven to 425°F.

MAKE THE CHERRY COMPOTE: Combine the ¼ cup sugar and the cherries in a medium saucepan. Cook over medium-high heat, stirring often, until thick and syrupy, 15 to 18 minutes. Stir in the almond extract and lemon juice.

PARBAKE THE CRUST: Stretch and pat the dough into a 10- to 11-inch round and put on a baking sheet. Brush with the butter and sprinkle with 1 tablespoon of the sugar. Bake until golden brown all over, 10 to 12 minutes.

TOP AND FINISH BAKING: Spread the cherry compote on the pizza crust and sprinkle the chocolate chips over the top. Return to the oven to lightly melt the chocolate, about 1 minute. Whip the cream with the remaining tablespoon sugar until soft peaks form. Serve slices of the pizza right away, topped with the whipped cream.

WARM SALTED CARAMEL
BANANA PUDDING

A still-warm, made-from-scratch pudding gets a modern twist with a salted caramel banana topping. To make this ahead of time, refrigerate the pudding and serve it chilled; caramelize the bananas when ready to serve.

¾ cup **sugar**

2½ tablespoons **cornstarch**

2¼ cups **milk**

3 large **egg yolks**, lightly beaten

2 teaspoons **vanilla extract**

4 tablespoons (½ stick) **unsalted butter**

2 medium **bananas**, sliced crosswise about ¼ inch thick

½ teaspoon **kosher salt**

MAKE THE PUDDING: Whisk ¼ cup of the sugar and the cornstarch in a medium saucepan. Whisk in ¼ cup of the milk and the egg yolks until smooth. Whisk in the remaining 2 cups milk and bring to a boil over medium-high heat, stirring and scraping the bottom and corners of the pan often with a heatproof rubber spatula. Boil, stirring constantly, until thick, about 2 minutes. Remove from the heat and whisk in the vanilla and 1 tablespoon of the butter. Divide the pudding among 4 glasses or dessert cups.

CARAMELIZE THE BANANAS: Combine the remaining ½ cup sugar with 2 tablespoons water in a medium skillet; stir to moisten all of the sugar. Cook over medium-high heat, swirling the skillet so the sugar cooks evenly, until dark golden brown, 5 to 7 minutes. Add the remaining 3 tablespoons butter, the bananas, and salt and cook, stirring, until the bananas are slightly softened, about 2 minutes.

SERVE: Spoon the bananas on top of the pudding and serve warm.

SERVES 4

ACTIVE TIME

10 minutes

TOTAL TIME

20 minutes

THIN LEMON PANCAKES WITH SWEETENED SOUR CREAM AND BLUEBERRIES

A cross between a traditional pancake and a crêpe, this almost all-pantry dessert is on your table in around 20 minutes.

⅔ cup **milk**

6 tablespoons **all-purpose flour**

4 tablespoons **granulated sugar**

2 teaspoons grated **lemon zest**

Kosher salt

2 large **eggs**

⅔ cup **sour cream**

2 teaspoons fresh **lemon juice**

2 tablespoons **unsalted butter**

1 cup **blueberries**

Confectioners' sugar, for dusting

MAKE THE PANCAKE BATTER: Mix the milk, flour, 2 tablespoons of the granulated sugar, the lemon zest, a large pinch of salt, and the eggs in a blender.

WHISK THE SWEETENED CREAM: Whisk the sour cream, lemon juice, a pinch of salt, and the remaining 2 tablespoons granulated sugar.

COOK THE PANCAKES: Heat 1 tablespoon of the butter in a large nonstick skillet over medium heat. Pour half of the batter into the skillet and cook until set, without flipping, 2 to 4 minutes. Gently slide onto a plate. Make another pancake with the remaining butter and batter. Cut each pancake in half and set on a dessert plate.

SERVE: Dollop sweetened cream onto the pancake halves. Top with the blueberries and fold into triangles. Sprinkle with confectioners' sugar and serve.

SERVES 4

ACTIVE TIME

10 minutes

TOTAL TIME

1 hour
15 minutes
(includes
freezing time)

CHILE AFFOGATO

Good old vanilla meets hot coffee and the warming spices of Mexico for a comforting and sophisticated dessert.

1 pint **vanilla ice cream**

¾ teaspoon ground **cinnamon**

½ teaspoon **chile powder**

¼ teaspoon **cayenne**

½ cup **heavy cream**

¾ cup **hot espresso** or **strong coffee**

FLAVOR THE ICE CREAM: Let the ice cream soften slightly, then work in the cinnamon, chile powder, and cayenne. Freeze until solid, about 1 hour.

SERVE: Beat the cream to soft peaks. Divide the ice cream among bowls and pour the espresso over the ice cream. Top with the whipped cream and serve immediately.

MAKE IT ICY

For a hot-weather treat, float the **spicy ice cream** in **iced coffee, cream soda,** or a mixture of the two—or a creamy Irish **stout** (chocolate stout or oatmeal stout if you can find it). Garnish with **crushed pretzels, corn nuts,** plain or chocolate puffed **rice cereal,** or **caramel popcorn.**

SERVES
6 TO 8;
MAKES 16
BROWNIES

ACTIVE TIME

10 minutes

TOTAL TIME

35 minutes

MOCHA BROWNIES WITH COFFEE AND CINNAMON

Fudgy brownie lovers, this is for you: brownies for grown-ups, with a strong coffee kick.

12 tablespoons (1½ sticks) **unsalted butter**, plus more for the pan
1 cup **sugar**
¾ cup **unsweetened cocoa powder**
2 teaspoons **instant coffee**
½ teaspoon ground **cinnamon**
1 teaspoon **vanilla extract**
¼ teaspoon **kosher salt**
2 large **eggs**
⅓ cup **all-purpose flour**

SET UP: Preheat the oven to 325°F. Butter a 9-inch square baking pan.

MAKE THE BATTER: Combine the butter, sugar, cocoa powder, coffee, cinnamon, vanilla, and salt in a medium saucepan over medium heat. Stir until well combined, then remove from the heat and let cool to warm. Beat in the eggs, one at a time, until the batter is glossy and smooth. Stir in the flour until combined.

BAKE THE BROWNIES: Pour the batter into the prepared pan and bake until the brownies are set, 20 to 25 minutes. Let cool in the pan, then cut into 16 squares.

SHORTBREAD
COOKIES

MARKET BASKET

Speedy dessert without resorting to ice cream? Basic ingredients that you probably already have on hand turn into cheesecakes, parfait, and a deliciously sweet and salty pretzel pie.

EACH RECIPE SERVES 4 TO 6

STRAWBERRIES

SLICED
ALMONDS

CREAM CHEESE

MINI CHOCOLATE-STRAWBERRY CHEESECAKES

Pulse 1 cup lightly crushed **shortbread cookies** with ½ cup **sliced almonds** and 3 tablespoons each melted **unsalted butter** and **granulated sugar** in a food processor until finely ground. Spray a muffin tin with **nonstick cooking spray.** Press the crumbs on the bottom and sides of 6 muffin cups. Bake at 375°F until golden, about 10 minutes. Heat 3 ounces chopped **semisweet chocolate** in a large bowl in the microwave, stirring every 30 seconds until just melted. Add ½ cup **confectioners' sugar,** 5 ounces softened **cream cheese,** and 3 tablespoons **heavy cream,** and beat to combine with an electric mixer. Spoon into the muffin cups and refrigerate until set, about 20 minutes. Macerate 1½ cups finely diced **strawberries** in 2 tablespoons granulated sugar until syrupy, about 15 minutes. Unmold cheesecakes and serve topped with the strawberries. TOTAL TIME: 1 HOUR 10 MINUTES

STRAWBERRY PARFAIT WITH NUTTY CRUMBLE

Toss ⅓ cup each crushed **shortbread cookies, sliced almonds,** and **corn flakes** with 1 tablespoon each **granulated sugar** and melted **unsalted butter** on a baking sheet. Bake at 375°F until golden brown, about 6 minutes. Puree 1 cup chopped **strawberries** in a blender with 2 tablespoons **confectioners' sugar** until smooth. Beat 6 ounces softened **cream cheese** and ¼ cup confectioners' sugar in a large bowl with an electric mixer until smooth and fluffy. Add 1¼ cups **heavy cream** and beat until it just holds stiff peaks. Drizzle 1 to 2 teaspoons strawberry puree in the bottom of 4 wineglasses. Fold the remaining puree into the cream; it's OK if there are some streaks. Spoon half of the cream into the wineglasses and sprinkle with half of the shortbread crumble. Top with the remaining cream, followed by the remaining crumble. TOTAL TIME: 25 MINUTES

STRAWBERRY SHORTBREAD PRETZEL PIE

Spray a 9-inch round cake or springform pan with **nonstick cooking spray** and line with parchment paper. Melt 3 tablespoons **unsalted butter** in a medium saucepan over medium heat. Add 2 cups **mini marshmallows** and stir until melted. Mix 1 cup crushed **shortbread cookies** with 1½ cups lightly crushed **pretzels.** Remove the saucepan from the heat and stir in the cookies and pretzels. Press evenly into the bottom of the prepared pan. Let cool, then remove from the pan, and transfer to a serving plate. Simmer 1 pound quartered **strawberries** with ¼ cup **sugar** until slightly broken down and thickened, 12 to 18 minutes (depending on ripeness). Cool slightly, then stir in 1 tablespoon fresh **lemon juice.** Beat 8 ounces softened **cream cheese** with ¼ cup sugar and 1 tablespoon fresh lemon juice until smooth. Spread evenly on the cookie round. Top with the strawberries, garnish with toasted **sliced almonds** and crushed pretzels and serve. TOTAL TIME: 45 MINUTES

SERVES 8

ACTIVE TIME

15 minutes

TOTAL TIME

4 hours
10 minutes

COCONUT PANNA COTTA
WITH CANDIED PEANUTS

Coconut milk and heavy cream combine into a wobbly and luscious dessert topped with a sweet, nutty crunch. The brittle is also especially good with macadamia nuts.

2 teaspoons **unflavored gelatin**

Vegetable oil, for the ramekins

1 (13- to 14-ounce) can **coconut milk**

1 cup **heavy cream**

½ cup plus ⅓ cup **sugar**

Kosher salt

½ cup **salted peanuts**

BLOOM THE GELATIN: Sprinkle the gelatin over ¼ cup water in a shallow bowl and let stand until softened, about 2 minutes.

MAKE THE PANNA COTTA: Oil eight 4-ounce ramekins. Heat the coconut milk, cream, the ½ cup sugar, and a pinch of salt in a small saucepan until hot but not simmering. Stir in the gelatin until dissolved. Divide the panna cotta among the prepared ramekins. Cover and refrigerate until set, at least 4 hours.

CANDY THE PEANUTS: Meanwhile, mix the ⅓ cup sugar with 3 to 4 teaspoons water (until the consistency of wet sand) in a heavy skillet over medium heat, swirling the skillet occasionally for even browning (do not stir the mixture), about 10 minutes. When the sugar is a deep caramel color, remove from the heat, stir in the peanuts, and immediately pour onto an ungreased sheet of aluminum foil; let cool completely.

SERVE: When ready to serve, run a sharp knife around the edge of the ramekins, then invert the panna cottas onto serving plates. Coarsely chop the peanut brittle and serve sprinkled over the top.

ACKNOWLEDGMENTS

This book wouldn't exist without all the chefs, judges, production staff, and programming team who make *Chopped* the show it is. Our thanks to them.

Food Network's president, Brooke Johnson; general managers, Sergei Kuharsky and Bob Tuschman; art director, Alanna Siviero; director of business affairs, Cory Greenberg; VP of research, Dave Schlieker; and Susie Fogelson, Amanda Melnick, and Laura Bernard in our marketing department provided invaluable support throughout the development process. Our partners at Clarkson Potter, Pam Krauss, Doris Cooper, Marysarah Quinn, Jane Treuhaft, and Rica Allannic and her team, helped shape the book every step of the way.

Our kitchen at Food Network houses an incredible range of passions and talents; the list of names to follow should be proof that too many cooks don't spoil the broth at all.

All the delicious recipe development (and arduous tasting) was overseen by Jill Novatt, along with Andrea Albin, Vincent Camillo, Treva Chadwell, Ian Knauer, Amanda Catrini, Sarah Balke, Rick Martinez, and Marite Acosta.

Rupa Bhattacharya and Heather Ramsdell gave the book its voice, along with Liz Tarpy, Katie Allen, Jenny Bierman, Leah Brickley, Danielle LaRosa, and Larisa Alvarez.

Mory Thomas directed Armando Rafael's gorgeous photography. Jeanne Lurvey was prop stylist. Morgan Hass was food stylist, supported by Richmond Flores and Mary Beth Bray.

Our operations team kept every ingredient at the ready and everything running smoothly: Dave Mechlowicz, Jake Schiffman, Athen Fleming, Richardo Scott, and Louis DeJesus.

And a very special thanks to Susan Stockton, who had the vision and heart to lead our culinary team for more than twenty years.

—KATHERINE ALFORD, SENIOR VICE PRESIDENT, FOOD NETWORK KITCHEN

INDEX

A

Affogato, chile, 228
African chicken and almond stew, 53
Almond(s): almond fried chicken with
    roasted kale and apples, 53
  almond wine pan sauce, 100–101
  and carrot arancini, 211
  and chicken stew, African, 53
  mayo, grilled chicken banh mi with
    pickled apple kale slaw and, 53
  toasted cauliflower with ham and,
    124
  and white wine mussels, 189
Apple(s): apple Dijon pan sauce,
    100–101
  cumin pork steak with grilled savoy
    cabbage and, 96–98
  and kale, roasted, almond fried
    chicken with, 53
  and oats meatloaf, 151
  pickled apple kale slaw, grilled
    chicken banh mi with almond
    mayo and, 53
Arancini, carrot and almond, 211
Arctic char, 184–85
Artichoke and spinach dip mac and
    cheese, 21
Arugula: bulgur vegetable pilaf, 206
  salad, grilled chicken tonnato with,
    60–61
Asian salad dressing, 167
Asian vinaigrette, spicy, 166
Asparagus: roasted shrimp cocktail
    salad, 173
Avocado: avocado buttermilk dressing,
    tuna and potato salad with, 170
  Bibb Cobb salad, 161
  mayo, green bean tempura with, 130

B

Bacon: bacon-citrus vinaigrette, 166
  Bibb Cobb salad, 161
  and blue cheese, grilled lettuce
    wedge with, 133
  shrimp ramen, 193
  spaghetti with tomato carbonara, 19
Banana salted caramel pudding, warm,
    225
Banh mi, grilled chicken, with almond
    mayo and pickled apple kale slaw,
    53

Barley, 202
  casserole, scalloped, 200
Basil-balsamic vinaigrette, 166
BBQ sauce, peach pickle, grilled
    chicken with, 58–59
Beans. See also Green bean(s)
  cauliflower and cannellini mash, 124
  nacho bake, 78
  quick skillet kielbasa pork and beans,
    106–7
  refried white beans, salsa-marinated
    skirt steak soft tacos with, 85–86
  spicy taco salad, 164
Beef. See also Steak
  beef picadillo enchiladas, 141
  Cajun spiced burgers, 143
  meat and collards pizza, 152–53
  meatloaf variations, 151
  Mexican hero sandwiches, 86
  pot roast, 108–9
  quick pan sauces for, 100–101
  shepherd's stew with dumplings, 149
Beer: Mexican beer pan sauce, 100–101
  and onion pot roast, 109
Beet(s), 114, 117
  and red cabbage slaw, 117
  roasted beet and orange salad with
    beet greens and walnuts, 117
  salt-roasted, with horseradish sour
    cream, 117
Bell peppers. See Pepper(s)
Bibb Cobb salad, 161
Big Easy eggs benedict, 191
Biscuits, oat and whole-grain, 207
Black Forest dessert pizza, 222
Blueberries, thin lemon pancakes with
    sour cream and, 226
Blue cheese: and bacon, grilled lettuce
    wedge with, 133
  Bibb Cobb salad, 161
  salad dressing, 167
Broccoli, 114, 120
  braised, with chickpeas and olives,
    120
  and Cheddar frittata, 73
  pork and egg stir-fry with, 144–45
  Southeast Asian charred, 120
  toasted couscous broccoli slaw with
    buttermilk dressing, 120
Broccoli rabe: Philly-style garlicky
    greens and egg sandwich, 74–75

Brown butter sauce, New Orleans,
    broiled trout with, 190–91
Brownies, mocha, with coffee and
    cinnamon, 229
Brown rice. See Rice
Brussels sprouts, 114, 119
  creamed, 119
  roasted, with salami, potatoes, and
    onions, 119
  shaved raw, with red peppers,
    peanuts, and sweet chile dressing,
    119
Buffalo sautéed Romaine lettuce, 133
Bulgur, 202
  bulgur vegetable pilaf, 206
Burgers, Cajun spiced, 143
Buttermilk: avocado buttermilk
    dressing, tuna and potato salad
    with, 170
  buttermilk-herb salad dressing, 167
  dressing, toasted couscous broccoli
    slaw with, 120
Butternut squash, 114, 136
  butternut coconut curry, 136
  sausage-stuffed butternut roast,
    136
  shaved butternut squash salad, 136
  turkey hand pies with kale and, 156

C

Cabbage: beet and red cabbage slaw,
    117
  cumin pork steak with grilled savoy
    cabbage and apples, 96–98
Caesar potato salad, easy, 132
Caesar salad dressing, 167
Cajun spiced burgers, 143
Cannellini bean and cauliflower mash,
    124
Capers, orecchiette with garlic, bread
    crumbs, and, 20
Caponata, pepper, 118
Caramel: warm salted caramel banana
    pudding, 225
Carpaccio, cremini, 129
Carrot(s), 114, 123
  and almond arancini, 211
  curried roasted vegetable and
    couscous salad, 174
  lemon roasted, 123
  maple-glazed, 123

Carrot(s) (*continued*)
  roasted carrot and onion risotto, 212–13
  salad, Moroccan, 123
Casserole: barley, scalloped, 200
  char noodle, with cress salad, 185
  pizza strata, 65
  skillet spaghetti, 66
Catfish, Moroccan spice blackened, 183
Cauliflower, 115, 124
  and cannellini bean mash, 124
  curried roasted vegetable and couscous salad, 174
  grilled cauliflower steak with tomato relish, 124
  toasted, with ham and almonds, 124
Celery, 115, 125
  and cherry tomatoes, broiled, with shaved Parmesan, 125
  jerk chicken, sausage, and celery fricassee, 56
  and leeks, braised, with vanilla, 125
  sliced raw celery salad with melon and lemon dressing, 125
Char, 184–85
Cheddar: and broccoli frittata, 73
  Cheddar kale soufflé, 71
  nacho bake, 78
  scalloped barley casserole, 200
  tomato-Cheddar gratin, 135
Cheese. *See also* Blue cheese; Cheddar; Cream cheese; Goat cheese; Parmesan; Pasta
  cheesy salsa meatloaf, 151
  disco balls, 147
  ham and peas frittata, 73
  Mexican hero sandwiches, 86
  and mushroom baked polenta, 217
  pizza strata, 65
  and spinach stuffed chicken breasts, with herbed nuts, 46–47
Cheesecakes, mini chocolate-strawberry, 231
Cherries: Black Forest dessert pizza, 222
Chicken, 39–61
  almond fried, with roasted kale and apples, 53
  and almond stew, spicy African, 53
  Bibb Cobb salad, 161
  breasts, spinach and cheese stuffed, with herbed nuts, 46–47
  chilled peanut chicken noodle salad, 32–34
  Greek-spiced wings and potatoes with yogurt dipping sauce, 44
  grilled: banh mi, with almond mayo and pickled apple kale slaw, 53; with peach pickle BBQ sauce,

58–59; sandwich, with parsley pesto, 54–55; tonnato, with arugula salad, 60–61
  jerk chicken, sausage, and celery fricassee, 56
  Moroccan chicken and lemon with date couscous, 48–50
  quick pan sauces for, 100–101
  roasted chicken Provençal, 57
  sautéed, with quick mole sauce and cilantro rice, 41–43
  Singapore chicken fried rice, 51
  tacos, Turkish, 157
Chickpeas: and olives, braised broccoli with, 120
  roasted corn and chickpea salad, 126
Chile affogato, 228
Chocolate: Black Forest dessert pizza, 222
  melted ice cream chocolate mousse, 221
  mini chocolate-strawberry cheesecakes, 231
  mocha brownies with coffee and cinnamon, 229
Chorizo: and chicken brown rice paella, 214–15
  nacho bake, 78
Chowder, char-corn-cress, with wonton crackers, 185
Cilantro rice, sautéed chicken with quick mole sauce and, 41–43
Citrus-bacon vinaigrette, 166
Cobb salad, Bibb, 161
Coconut: butternut coconut curry, 136
  coconut creamed corn, 126
  and green bean stir-fry, 130
  panna cotta, with candied peanuts, 233
Coffee: chile affogato, 228
  mocha brownies with cinnamon and, 229
Cognac horseradish cream sauce, 100–101
Collards and meat pizza, 152–53
Corn, 115, 126
  char-corn-cress chowder with wonton crackers, 185
  on the cob, with sweet and spicy yogurt sauce, 126
  coconut creamed corn, 126
  ravioli, with cress pesto and char, 185
  roasted corn and chickpea salad, 126
Cornmeal, 202. *See also* Polenta
Couscous: curried roasted vegetable and couscous salad, 174
  date, Moroccan chicken and lemon with, 48–50

toasted couscous broccoli slaw with buttermilk dressing, 120
Cream cheese: Alfredo, tortellini with peas and, 28
  strawberry desserts with, 231
Cremini mushrooms, 115, 129. *See also* Mushroom(s)
Cress. *See* Watercress
Cumin pork steak with grilled savoy cabbage and apples, 96–98
Curried roasted vegetable and couscous salad, 174
Curry, butternut coconut, 136

D
Desserts, 219–33
  Black Forest dessert pizza, 222
  chile affogato, 228
  coconut panna cotta with candied peanuts, 233
  melted ice cream chocolate mousse, 221
  mini chocolate-strawberry cheesecakes, 231
  mocha brownies with coffee and cinnamon, 229
  strawberry parfait with nutty crumble, 231
  strawberry shortbread pretzel pie, 231
  thin lemon pancakes with sour cream and blueberries, 226
  warm salted caramel banana pudding, 225
Dill: lemon dill pan sauce, 100–101
  salad dressings, 167
Disco balls, 147
Dumplings, shepherd's stew with, 149

E
Eggplant: eggplant yogurt sauce, farfalle with, 37
  quinoa shrimp fried "rice", 204–5
Egg(s), 63–81
  Bibb Cobb salad, 161
  Big Easy eggs benedict, 191
  Cheddar kale soufflé, 71
  frittata variations, 72–73
  and garlicky greens sandwich, Philly-style, 74–75
  meat and potatoes quiche, 68
  nacho bake, 78
  pizza strata, 65
  poached in martini marinara, 77
  and pork stir-fry with broccoli, 144–45
  prosciutto-pesto coddled egg cups, 81
  quinoa shrimp fried "rice", 204–5

skillet spaghetti casserole, 66
Swiss chard baked eggs, 69
Enchiladas, beef picadillo, 141

F
Farfalle with eggplant yogurt sauce, 37
Farro, 202
  three-onion farro soup, 199
Fennel pot roast, Italian, 109
Fish, 177–95. *See also* Tuna
  broiled trout with New Orleans
    brown butter sauce, 190–91
  char-corn-cress chowder with
    wonton crackers, 185
  char noodle casserole with cress
    salad, 185
  corn ravioli with cress pesto and
    char, 185
  marinated tilapia tacos, 180
  Moroccan spice blackened catfish,
    183
  quick pan sauces for, 100–101
  slow-cooked salmon with olive-
    bread crumb sprinkle, 186
  super-sauce grilled salmon with
    grilled scallions, 188
  tilapia tartar cakes, 179
Frittata variations, 72–73

G
Garlic: garlic-herb salad dressing, 167
  garlicky greens and egg sandwich,
    Philly-style, 74–75
  orecchiette with capers, bread
    crumbs, and, 20
  sweet vinegar garlic pan sauce,
    100–101
  and vinegar glazed pork chops with
    scallions, 104–5
Ginger-sesame vinaigrette, 166
Goat cheese: mushroom goat cheese
    pan sauce, 100–101
  vinaigrette, 166
Goulash pot roast, 109
Grains, 197–217. *See also* Couscous;
    Quinoa; Rice; Risotto
  basic cooking methods, 201–3
  bulgur vegetable pilaf, 206
  mushroom and cheese baked
    polenta, 217
  oat and whole-grain biscuits, 207
  recipe list, 198
  scalloped barley casserole, 200
  three-onion farro soup, 199
Gratin, tomato-Cheddar, 135
Greek bell pepper salad, 118
Greek-spiced chicken wings and
    potatoes with yogurt dipping
    sauce, 44

Green bean(s), 115, 130
  and coconut stir-fry, 130
  and kale, Southern stewed, 130
  tempura, with avocado mayo, 130
Greens. *See also specific types*
  garlicky greens and egg sandwich,
    Philly-style, 74–75
Ground meats and poultry, 139–57. *See
    also* Meatballs; Pasta; Sausage;
    specific meats
  recipe list, 140
Gyros, Italian, with yogurt and tomato,
    93

H
Ham: and peas frittata, 73
  Serrano, toasted cauliflower with
    almonds and, 124
  tortellini with cream-cheese Alfredo
    and peas, 28
Hamburgers, Cajun spiced, 143
Hand pies, turkey, with butternut
    squash and kale, 156
Herbs, 14, 15. *See also specific types*
  buttermilk-herb salad dressing,
    167
  garlic-herb salad dressing, 167
  grape tomato-herb sauce, 27
  herbed nuts, spinach and cheese
    stuffed chicken breasts with,
    46–47
  herb vinaigrette, 166
Horseradish, 173
  Cognac horseradish cream sauce,
    100–101
  horseradish sour cream, salt-roasted
    beets with, 117

I
Ice cream: chile affogato, 228
  melted ice cream chocolate mousse,
    221
Italian fennel pot roast, 109
Italian gyros with yogurt and tomato,
    93
Italian vinaigrette, 166

J
Jerk chicken, sausage, and celery
    fricassee, 56

K
Kale: and apples, roasted, almond fried
    chicken with, 53
  Cheddar kale soufflé, 71
  and green beans, Southern stewed,
    130
  nutty tropical kale and rice salad,
    162

pickled apple kale slaw, grilled
    chicken banh mi with almond
    mayo and, 53
  turkey hand pies with butternut
    squash and, 156
Kielbasa pork and beans, quick, 106–7

L
Lamb: shepherd's stew with dumplings,
    149
Leeks and celery, braised, with vanilla,
    125
Lemon: lemon dill pan sauce, 100–101
  lemon roasted carrots, 123
  lemony ricotta sauce, 27
  lemony spaghetti and zucchini, 137
  and melon dressing, sliced raw
    celery salad with, 125
  Moroccan chicken and, with date
    couscous, 48–50
  pancakes, with sour cream and
    blueberries, 226
Lettuce, 115, 133. *See also* Salad(s)
  buffalo sautéed Romaine, 133
  grilled wedge with bacon and blue
    cheese, 133
  lettuce soup, 133
  roasted shrimp cocktail salad, 173
  Thai turkey lettuce wraps, 155
Linguine with bell pepper marinara, 35

M
Mac and cheese, spinach and artichoke
    dip, 21
Mango: nutty tropical kale and rice
    salad, 162
Maple-glazed carrots, 123
Marinara: bell pepper, linguine with, 35
  martini, eggs poached in, 77
  quick and easy, 27
Mayonnaise: almond, grilled chicken
    banh mi with pickled apple kale
    slaw and, 53
  avocado, green bean tempura with,
    130
  creamy salad dressings, 167
Meat. *See also specific types*
  meat and potatoes quiche, 68
Meatballs: disco balls, 147
  pork barbecue meatball sandwiches,
    146–47
  spaghetti and, Mexican, 22–24
Meatloaf, 150–51
Melon and lemon dressing, sliced raw
    celery salad with, 125
Mexican beer pan sauce, 100–101
Mexican hero sandwiches, 86
Mexican spaghetti and meatballs,
    22–24

Millet, 202
Mint and tuna pasta, 27
Mocha brownies with coffee and
    cinnamon, 229
Mole sauce, quick, sautéed chicken
    with cilantro rice and, 41–43
Moroccan carrot salad, 123
Moroccan chicken and lemon, with
    date couscous, 48–50
Moroccan spice blackened catfish, 183
Mushroom(s), 115
    broiled trout with New Orleans
        brown butter sauce, 190–91
    and cheese baked polenta, 217
    cremini carpaccio, 129
    crispy, rigatoni with spicy sausage
        and, 31
    mushroom goat cheese pan sauce,
        100–101
    quick pickled baby cremini, 129
    red wine mushroom sauce, strip
        steak with, 88–89
    shrimp ramen, 193
    stir-fried, with ketchup-ginger sauce,
        129
Mussels, almond and white wine, 189
Mustard: apple Dijon pan sauce,
    100–101
    mustard pickle pan sauce, 100–101
    pretzel-mustard-crusted pork
        tenderloin sliders, 102–3
    smashed potatoes, strip steak with
        red-wine mushroom sauce and,
        88–89

N
Nacho bake, 78
New Orleans brown butter sauce,
    broiled trout with, 190–91
Noodles. See also Pasta
    char noodle casserole with cress
        salad, 185
    chilled peanut chicken noodle salad,
        32–34
    parsley, butter-basted flat iron steak
        with tomato butter sauce and,
        91–92
    shrimp ramen, 193
Nuts. See also Almond(s); Peanuts;
    Walnuts
    nutty tropical kale and rice salad, 162
    toasted spiced, broiled paprika flank
        steak with, 94–95

O
Oats: oat and whole-grain biscuits,
    207
    oats and apple meatloaf, 151
Old-fashioned pan sauce, 100–101

Olives: and chickpeas, braised broccoli
    with, 120
    martini marinara, eggs poached in,
        77
    olive-bread crumb sprinkle, slow-
        cooked salmon with, 186
    roasted chicken Provençal, 57
Onions. See also Scallions
    beer and onion pot roast, 109
    roasted Brussels sprouts with salami,
        potatoes, and, 119
    roasted carrot and onion risotto,
        212–13
    three-onion farro soup, 199
Orange: bacon-citrus vinaigrette, 166
    and roasted beet salad, with beet
        greens and walnuts, 117
Orecchiette with garlic, capers, and
    bread crumbs, 20

P
Paella, chorizo and chicken brown rice,
    214–15
Pancakes: lemon, with sour cream and
    blueberries, 226
    skillet potato pancakes, 132
Pan-cooked meats, 83–109. See also
    specific meats
    quick sauces for, 99–101
    recipe list, 84
Panna cotta, coconut, with candied
    peanuts, 233
Pantry ingredients, 12–15
Panzanella, Chopped, 169
Paprika flank steak, broiled, with
    toasted spiced nuts, 94–95
Parfait, strawberry, with nutty crumble,
    231
Parmesan, 125. See also Pasta
    Parmesan sour cream, blistered
        cherry tomatoes with toasted
        bread and, 135
    shaved, broiled celery and cherry
        tomatoes with, 125
Parsley: noodles, butter-basted flat
    iron steak with tomato butter
    sauce and, 91–92
    pesto, grilled chicken sandwich with,
        54–55
Pasta, 17–37. See also Noodles
    cheese and pepper, classic, 27
    corn ravioli with cress pesto and
        char, 185
    farfalle with eggplant yogurt sauce,
        37
    grape tomato-herb sauce, 27
    lemony ricotta sauce, 27
    lemony spaghetti and zucchini, 137
    linguine with bell pepper marinara, 35

Mexican spaghetti and meatballs,
    22–24
    orecchiette with garlic, capers, and
        bread crumbs, 20
    penne alla Mary, 25
    quick and easy marinara sauce, 27
    rigatoni with spicy sausage and
        crispy mushrooms, 31
    spaghetti with tomato carbonara, 19
    spinach and artichoke dip mac and
        cheese, 21
    tortellini with cream-cheese Alfredo
        and peas, 28
    tuna and mint, 27
Peach pickle BBQ sauce, grilled
    chicken with, 58–59
Peanuts: candied, coconut panna cotta
    with, 233
    chilled peanut chicken noodle salad,
        32–34
    shaved raw Brussels sprouts with
        red peppers, sweet chile dressing,
        and, 119
    stuffed peppers with wheat berries,
        209–10
Peas: ham and peas frittata, 73
    tortellini with cream-cheese Alfredo
        and, 28
Penne alla Mary, 25
Pepper(s), 114, 118
    Greek bell pepper salad, 118
    linguine with bell pepper marinara,
        35
    pepper caponata, 118
    and pork stir-fry, 105
    and quinoa salad, 118
    red, shaved raw Brussels sprouts
        with peanuts, sweet chile dressing,
        and, 119
    Spanish potato chip frittata, 73
    stuffed, with wheat berries, 209–10
Pesto: cress, corn ravioli with char and,
    185
    parsley, grilled chicken sandwich
        with, 54–55
    prosciutto-pesto coddled egg cups,
        81
Pickled apple kale slaw, grilled chicken
    banh mi with, 53
Pickled baby cremini, quick, 129
Pickled salad dressing, 167
Pico de gallo stacks, 135
Pilaf, 201
    bulgur vegetable, 206
Pizza: Black Forest dessert pizza, 222
    meat and collards, 152–53
Pizza strata, 65
Polenta, 202
    mushroom and cheese baked, 217

Pomegranate pan sauce, 100–101
Pork. *See also* Bacon; Ham; Sausage
  chops, garlic and vinegar glazed,
    with scallions, 104–5
  cumin pork steak with grilled savoy
    cabbage and apples, 96–98
  and egg stir-fry with broccoli,
    144–45
  meatloaf variations, 151
  and pepper stir-fry, 105
  pork barbecue meatball sandwiches,
    146–47
  pot roast, 108–9
  pretzel-mustard-crusted pork
    tenderloin sliders, 102–3
  quick pan sauces for, 100–101
Potato chip frittata, Spanish, 73
Potatoes, 115, 132
  buttery roasted, with wilted spinach,
    132
  easy Caesar potato salad, 132
  Greek-spiced chicken wings and,
    with yogurt dipping sauce, 44
  meat and potatoes quiche, 68
  mustard smashed, strip steak with
    red wine mushroom sauce and,
    88–89
  roasted Brussels sprouts with salami,
    onions, and, 119
  skillet potato pancakes, 132
  tuna and roasted potato salad with
    avocado buttermilk dressing, 170
  twice-baked, spinach and cheese
    stuffed, 47
Pot roast, 108–9
Pretzel-mustard-crusted pork
    tenderloin sliders, 102–3
Pretzel pie, strawberry shortbread,
    231
Prosciutto-pesto coddled egg cups,
    81
Pudding, warm salted caramel banana,
    225

Q
Quiche, meat and potatoes, 68
Quinoa, 202
  and pepper salad, 118
  quinoa shrimp fried "rice," 204–5
  tangy quinoa meatloaf, 151

R
Ramen, shrimp, 193
Ravioli, corn, with cress pesto and char,
    185
Red peppers. *See* Pepper(s)
Red wine mushroom sauce, strip steak
    with mustard smashed potatoes
    and, 88–89

Rice. *See also* Risotto
  basic cooking methods, 201, 203
  chorizo and chicken brown rice
    paella, 214–15
  cilantro, sautéed chicken with quick
    mole sauce and, 41–43
  nutty tropical kale and rice salad, 162
  Singapore chicken fried rice, 51
  stuffed peppers with wheat berries,
    209–10
Ricotta sauce, lemony, 27
Rigatoni with spicy sausage and crispy
    mushrooms, 31
Risotto, 201, 203
  carrot and almond arancini, 211
  roasted carrot and onion, 212–13
Romaine lettuce, 115, 133. *See also*
    Lettuce; Salad(s)

S
Salad(s), 159–75. *See also* Slaw
  arugula, grilled chicken tonnato with,
    60–61
  Bibb Cobb salad, 161
  Caesar potato, easy, 132
  celery, sliced raw, with melon and
    lemon dressing, 125
  Chopped panzanella, 169
  cremini carpaccio, 129
  curried roasted vegetable and
    couscous, 174
  dressings and vinaigrettes for,
    165–67
  Greek bell pepper salad, 118
  Moroccan carrot salad, 123
  nutty tropical kale and rice, 162
  peanut chicken noodle, chilled,
    32–34
  pepper and quinoa, 118
  pepper caponata, 118
  pico de gallo stacks, 135
  roasted beet and orange, with beet
    greens and walnuts, 117
  roasted corn and chickpea, 126
  roasted shrimp cocktail salad, 173
  shaved butternut squash, 136
  shaved raw Brussels sprouts with red
    peppers, peanuts, and sweet chile
    dressing, 119
  spicy taco salad, 164
  tuna and roasted potato, with
    avocado buttermilk dressing, 170
  watercress, char noodle casserole
    with, 185
Salami: Chopped panzanella, 169
  roasted Brussels sprouts with
    potatoes, onions, and, 119
Salmon: slow-cooked, with olive-bread
    crumb sprinkle, 186

super-sauce grilled salmon with
    grilled scallions, 188
Salsa: cheesy salsa meatloaf, 151
  salsa-marinated skirt steak soft
    tacos with refried white beans,
    85–86
Salt-roasted beets with horseradish
    sour cream, 117
Sandwich(es). *See also* Burgers; Sliders
  Connecticut-Cajun shrimp rolls,
    194–95
  garlicky greens and egg, Philly-style,
    74–75
  grilled chicken banh mi with almond
    mayo and pickled apple kale slaw,
    53
  grilled chicken, with parsley pesto,
    54–55
  Mexican heroes, 86
  pork barbecue meatball, 146–47
Sauce(s). *See also* Pasta
  ketchup-ginger, mushrooms with,
    129
  martini marinara, eggs poached in,
    77
  mole, quick, sautéed chicken with,
    41–43
  New Orleans brown butter, broiled
    trout with, 190–91
  pantry sauces, 15
  peach pickle BBQ sauce, grilled
    chicken with, 58–59
  quick pan sauces, 99–101
  red wine mushroom, strip steak with,
    88–89
  yogurt dipping sauce, Greek-spiced
    wings and potatoes with, 44
  yogurt, sweet and spicy, corn on the
    cob with, 126
Sausage. *See also* Chorizo
  Italian gyros with yogurt and tomato,
    93
  jerk chicken, sausage, and celery
    fricassee, 56
  meat and potatoes quiche, 68
  quick skillet kielbasa pork and beans,
    106–7
  sausage-stuffed butternut roast, 136
  spicy, rigatoni with crispy
    mushrooms and, 31
Savoy cabbage and apples, grilled,
    cumin pork steak with, 96–98
Scallions: garlic and vinegar glazed
    pork chops with, 104–5
  grilled, super-sauce grilled salmon
    with, 188
Seafood. *See* Fish; Mussels; Shrimp
Shepherd's stew with dumplings, 149
Sherry-shallot vinaigrette, 166

Shrimp: Connecticut-Cajun shrimp
  rolls, 194–95
  Low Country shrimp frittata, 73
  quinoa shrimp fried "rice," 204–5
  roasted shrimp cocktail salad, 173
  shrimp ramen, 193
Singapore chicken fried rice, 51
Skillet spaghetti casserole, 66
Slaw: beet and red cabbage, 117
  pickled apple kale, grilled chicken
    banh mi with almond mayo and,
    53
  toasted couscous broccoli slaw with
    buttermilk dressing, 120
Sliders, pretzel-mustard-crusted pork
  tenderloin, 102–3
Soufflé, Cheddar kale, 71
Soup(s): Asian chicken noodle, 34
  char-corn-cress chowder with
    wonton crackers, 185
  lettuce soup, 133
  shrimp ramen, 193
  three-onion farro soup, 199
Southeast Asian charred broccoli, 120
Spaghetti: Mexican spaghetti and
    meatballs, 22–24
  simple sauces for, 27
  skillet spaghetti casserole, 66
  with tomato carbonara, 19
  and zucchini, lemony, 137
Spanish potato chip frittata, 73
Spices, 15
Spinach: and cheese stuffed chicken
    breasts, with herbed nuts, 46–47
  spinach and artichoke dip mac and
    cheese, 21
  wilted, buttery roasted potatoes
    with, 132
Squash. See Butternut squash;
  Zucchini
Steak: broiled paprika flank steak with
    toasted spiced nuts, 94–95
  butter-basted flat iron steak with
    tomato butter sauce and parsley
    noodles, 91–92
  cumin pork steak with grilled savoy
    cabbage and apples, 96–98
  quick pan sauces for, 99–101
  salsa-marinated skirt steak soft
    tacos with refried white beans,
    85–86
  strip steak with red wine mushroom
    sauce and mustard smashed
    potatoes, 88–89
Stew(s). See also Soup(s)
  African chicken and almond, spicy,
    53
  quick skillet kielbasa pork and beans,
    106–7

shepherd's stew with dumplings, 149
Stir-fry(ies): green bean and coconut,
    130
  mushrooms with ketchup-ginger
    sauce, 129
  pork and egg, with broccoli, 144–45
  pork and pepper, 105
Strawberry(ies): mini chocolate-
    strawberry cheesecakes, 231
  parfait, with nutty crumble, 231
  strawberry shortbread pretzel pie,
    231
Swiss chard baked eggs, 69

T
Tacos: marinated tilapia, 180
  salsa-marinated skirt steak, with
    refried white beans, 85–86
  Turkish chicken, 157
Taco salad, spicy, 164
Tart, zucchini, 137
Tempura, green bean, with avocado
    mayo, 130
Thai turkey lettuce wraps, 155
Tilapia: marinated tilapia tacos, 180
  tilapia tartar cakes, 179
Tomato(es), 115, 135
  Bibb Cobb salad, 161
  blistered cherry tomatoes with
    Parmesan sour cream and toasted
    bread, 135
  broiled celery and cherry tomatoes
    with shaved Parmesan, 125
  Chopped panzanella, 169
  farfalle with eggplant yogurt sauce,
    37
  Italian gyros with yogurt and, 93
  pico de gallo stacks, 135
  pizza strata, 65
  relish, grilled cauliflower steak with,
    124
  roasted chicken Provençal, 57
  sauces: beef picadillo enchiladas,
    141; grape tomato-herb, 27; martini
    marinara, 77; penne alla Mary,
    25; quick and easy marinara, 27;
    rigatoni with spicy sausage and
    crispy mushrooms, 31; tomato
    butter sauce, 91–92; tomato
    carbonara, 19; tomato-chile, 22–24
    tomato-Cheddar gratin, 135
Tortellini with cream-cheese Alfredo
    and peas, 28
Tortilla chips: nacho bake, 78
Trout, broiled, with New Orleans brown
    butter sauce, 190–91
Tuna: grilled chicken tonnato with
    arugula salad, 60–61
  and mint pasta, 27

and roasted potato salad, with
    avocado buttermilk dressing, 170
Turkey: Chopped panzanella, 169
  hand pies, with butternut squash and
    kale, 156
  Thai turkey lettuce wraps, 155
Turkish chicken tacos, 157

V
Vanilla, braised celery and leeks with,
    125
Vegetables, 111–37. See also specific
    vegetables
  choosing and storing, 114–15
  recipe list, 112–13
Vinaigrettes, 165, 166
Vinegar, 14
  garlic and vinegar glazed pork chops
    with scallions, 104–5
  sweet vinegar garlic pan sauce,
    100–101
Vodka, penne alla Mary with, 25

W
Walnuts: herbed, spinach and cheese
    stuffed chicken breasts with,
    46–47
  roasted beet and orange salad with
    beet greens and, 117
Watercress: char-corn-cress chowder
    with wonton crackers, 185
  pesto, corn ravioli with char and, 185
  salad, char noodle casserole with,
    185
Wheat berries, 203
  stuffed peppers with, 209–10
Whole-grain and oat biscuits, 207
Wonton crackers, char-corn-cress
    chowder with, 185

Y
Yogurt: creamy salad dressings, 167
  dipping sauce, Greek-spiced chicken
    wings and potatoes with, 44
  farfalle with eggplant yogurt sauce,
    37
  Italian gyros with tomato and, 93
  sweet and spicy yogurt sauce, corn
    on the cob with, 126

Z
Zucchini, 115, 137
  lemony spaghetti and, 137
  wedges, grilled breaded, 137
  zucchini tart, 137